S0-BRI-106

DATE DUE

Demco, Inc. 38-293

SCSU
SEP 21 2004
WITHDRAWN
W.C. BULEY LIBRARY

Conquering InfoClutter

This book is dedicated to teachers everywhere who work tirelessly to make a difference in the lives of children. To my first teacher, my Mom, Marta Hart, who is an inspiration to all. To those close at home, my husband Brian and my little Danny and Patrick who teach me something new every day.

Meghan J. Ormiston
Foreword by Kathy Schrock

Conquering InfoClutter

**Timesaving
Technology
Solutions
for Teachers**

CORWIN PRESS
A Sage Publications Company
Thousand Oaks, California

Copyright © 2004 by Corwin Press

All rights reserved. When forms and sample documents are included, their use is authorized only by educators, local school sites, and/or noncommercial or nonprofit entities who have purchased the book. Except for that usage, no part of this book may be reproduced or utilized in any form or by any means, electronic or mechanical, including photocopying, recording, or by any information storage and retrieval system, without permission in writing from the publisher.

For information:

Corwin Press
A Sage Publications Company
2455 Teller Road
Thousand Oaks, California 91320
www.corwinpress.com

Sage Publications Ltd.
6 Bonhill Street
London EC2A 4PU
United Kingdom

Sage Publications India Pvt. Ltd.
B-42, Panchsheel Enclave
Post Box 4109
New Delhi 110 017 India

Printed in the United States of America

Library of Congress Cataloging-in-Publication Data
Ormiston, Meghan J.
Conquering infoclutter : timesaving technology solutions for teachers /
Meghan J. Ormiston.
        p. cm.
Includes bibliographical references and index.
ISBN 0-7619-3129-5 (Cloth) — ISBN 0-7619-3130-9 (Paper)
   1. Teachers-Time management. 2. Educational technology.
3. Information technology. I. Title.
LB2838.8.O76 2004
371.33—dc22   2003017021

This book is printed on acid-free paper.

04   05   06   07   10   9   8   7   6   5   4   3   2   1

Acquisitions Editor:	Jean Ward
Production Editor:	Sanford Robinson
Copy Editor:	Eugenia Orlandi
Typesetter:	C&M Digitals (P) Ltd.
Proofreader:	Nancy Lambert
Cover Designer:	Michael Dubowe

Contents

List of Figures (Credits)

Foreword

Infoclutter . . . a great term to describe the information overload we experience each day! In this book, Meghan J. Ormiston provides us with practical tips and tricks for learning to manage this information for a variety of purposes, from personal productivity to information literacy, for an audience of teachers, students, and parents.

As those of you know who have attended any of Meg's presentations, she is an engaging speaker with a keen sense of practicality. Meg has a willingness to share her experiences in the context of helping us all become better teachers and learners. She is not afraid to laugh at herself, and the information, tips, and tricks in this book are a result of Meg's experiences and the experiences of classroom teachers she has come in contact with trying to conquer the information explosion.

The ideas presented are easy to adapt to any grade level and teaching situation. One of my favorite chapters is the file management chapter, which presents a "digital filing cabinet" analogy for maintaining order with all of your documents. Another very useful chapter for teachers is the one dealing with the creation of technology assessments to truly measure both the content skills and technology skills acquired by students.

Each chapter is introduced with a self-assessment, which serves to set the tone for what is to come next, and ends with a post-assessment to sum things up. There are activities to try out for both teachers and students, essential questions for furthering discussion, and professional development tips to use when training educators. There are personal narratives throughout, told only as Meg can tell them—with humor, compassion, and truth!

Kathy Schrock
Creator, *Kathy Schrock's Guide for Educators*

Acknowledgments

For all the talented teachers who have shared their challenges and celebrations, I thank you. I could not have completed this book without the love and support of my immediate and extended families. They were right there cheering me on as I edited between baseball games or hockey periods. To the friends who are always there to share a laugh and a story, here are a few more. To my many mentors and guides who keep pushing me to the next level, you know who you are, and we need to get together for lunch.

A big thank you belongs to Alan November for believing in me and sharing his wisdom and wit. To Kathy Schrock, I thank you for keeping me focused on the needs of teachers. Thank you to my acquisitions editor Jean Ward who pushed me when I needed it and understood when family came first. To Ian Jukes, thanks for urging me to transform this book and get it done. Thank you to my dear friend and colleague Stephanie Delgrosso who has shared so much of herself, her talents and her great stories from the professional development classrooms. For all the rest that I have not mentioned by name, I will get to you next time.

Corwin Press thanks the following reviewers for their contributions:

Kathy Schrock
Administrator for Technology
Nauset Public Schools
Orleans MA

Mike Muir
Director of the Maine Center for Meaningful Engaged Learning and
Assistant Professor of Middle Level Education and Educational Technology
University of Maine at Farmington
Farmington, ME

Debbie Reagan
LaSalle County Regional Office of Education
Ottawa, IL

Mark Standley
University of Alaska Education Leadership Program
Fairbanks, Alaska

Linda Johnson
Principal,
Samuel Sewall Greeley School
Winnetka, IL

About the Author

Meghan J. Ormiston is an author, teacher, and internationally known speaker, curriculum consultant, and professional development expert. She specializes in technology integration and standards-based achievement growth in reading and mathematics.

Improving student learning is Meg's goal for every professional development session. For over 18 years, she has planned professional development programs that meet the needs of educators. A former classroom teacher and current school board member, Meg addresses a wide range of audiences at all levels from pre-K through higher education or college.

Meg recognizes the importance of helping teachers set high expectations and deliver curriculum aligned to standards. Her upbeat presentation style, classroom background, and practical examples make her highly credible and effective with teachers. Her wide range of experiences and examples enrich her writing and presentations.

Meg holds a master's degree in curriculum and instruction and uses current research and practical methods to help teachers improve teaching and learning in their classrooms.

1

Conquering
InfoClutter

Infoclutter is everywhere. A search engine can locate millions of search results for topics, textbooks, and support materials weigh more than a child in the classroom, and file drawers are overflowing. Your e-mail inbox has hundreds of messages, the Web page needs to be updated, and you need to start the multimedia presentation needed for next week. Your data is everywhere, but it is easier to type something again than locate the file. You are not alone; help is here.

The problem today is not getting information. Instead, it is how to limit the information, validate the information, and organize the information you need. Some say we are in the information age, while others complain of information overload. Whatever label you use, everyone needs to deal with infoclutter.

There is more information available to us than ever before, valid and otherwise. In the digital age, new skills are needed to validate the information and weed through the clutter. Information literacy skills are part of the new essential skills for learners of all ages.

Self-Assessment

Self-Assessment for Conquering InfoClutter: Where Are You Now?

1. How are you using technology in the classroom?

2. What new things would you like to learn?

3. What are "technology timewasters" that you have experienced?

4. Specifically, what skills do you need to develop?

5. What access do you have to technology in the classroom?

6. What support do you have to use technology?

Copyright © 2004 by Corwin Press, Inc. All rights reserved. Reprinted from *Conquering Infoclutter: Timesaving Technology Solutions for Teachers* by Meghan Ormiston. Thousand Oaks, CA: Corwin Press, www.corwinpress.com. Reproduction authorized only for the local school site that has purchased this book.

INFOCLUTTER: NEW TERM, OLD PROBLEM ■

There was no such term as "information management" when I started teaching almost twenty years ago. Back then we were managing information, but that was mainly print information. The textbooks drove instruction, and students recorded their work on paper. I have been through many a school bag since then, lugging around papers to be graded. With hindsight being twenty/twenty, things were easier back then!

Way back when I put up my first bulletin board, teachers and students were paper-trained. Classrooms were textbook driven. I made my share of "dittos" before we upgraded to a copy machine that worked well until about April when we ran out of paper! A few years later we were copying fools! The copy room was where you went to hear the news and wait in line for your turn to copy both sides and staple.

Not long after we all felt comfortable collating along came computers, and now cut and paste did not include glue. New discoveries were made in the computer lab including creating files, typing letters, and actually inserting clip art. All of these precious things could be saved to a large floppy disk slightly smaller than a forty-five rpm record.

With eyes wide open, we were ready for amazing things. I still remember the excitement of our grade level team when we could sit down, type a field trip letter, print the letter only to find a mistake, make corrections, and modify the letter in a matter of minutes. Back then this was a big deal!

There were some bumps along the way. Our precious floppies no longer fit in the new screaming-fast computers. We transferred some of the old data, but most went to the drawer. The next year we retyped the same field trip letter on the new machine. Soon we could save to the hard drive! Then a very carefully rigged "network" let more than one computer talk to the printer. Of course, everything needed to be printed and filed because of the frequent computer crashes.

We saved for a long time and bought our first home computer. It actually was a state-of-the-art portable computer. I needed a heavy-duty wheeled cart to carry it to and from school. This screaming-fast machine helped me fully explore the state-of-the-art software that came with it. I could even save to the hard drive, no comment on how small that was.

We formed a technology committee and spent hours talking about "next steps." We struggled to understand what a network was physically and why would we ever need to connect all the computers together. The Internet? A small group of us set out for training on how to connect to the Internet; back then this "configuration training for at-home use" took multiple sessions.

With new computers, networked, and connected to the Internet, we were living large! About then we celebrated the birth of our first son, born into a new networked world! Flash-forward to the classroom he now attends.

■ THE WIRED CLASSROOM TODAY

Classrooms today are different, even if they are housed in old buildings. Many classrooms are wired to the network and the world with high-speed connections that open a world of possibilities. From a teacher's perspective, this presents new challenges. Many students were born into a networked world. These students do not know the other world in which I started teaching.

Powerful new technology tools are in our classroom with the promise of transforming teaching and learning. In preparing and delivering lessons, there are so many options that it is hard to select the best way to present the information. Many teachers are expected to use technology, but teachers need new skills to sift through digital resources and organize those resources for instruction.

The sifting, organizing in a timesaving way, is why I wrote this book. There are so many options available. Teachers need a set of foundation skills to best use technology. Before we can jump to transforming lessons using technology, we need skills: a new digital foundation.

Professional Development

For educators, the sifting and organizing of the information needs to be in a way that saves time. A "new digital foundation" needs to be laid so that in moving forward each teacher has the skills to use information to improve instruction. Before we can race to integrate and transform curriculum, we need a new set of digital skills to make the most of the information available.

The focus is not on how the "boxes and wires" that make up the computer work, but on the information that flows with the help of the technology. With this focus on information and coupled with my work with teachers, I have identified what I think is holding so many people back when it comes to technology, that is infoclutter.

■ DEFINING INFOCLUTTER

Many of us have infoclutter. I define infoclutter as "information we have collected that is cluttering our lives." Although this term is yet to appear in the dictionary, I believe it is reaching epidemic proportions.

This infoclutter may include print materials, e-mail messages, on-line resources, books, letters, research, to-do lists, newspapers, television, and all the personal stacks and files of paper.

The infoclutter is wasting time! According to the American Demographic Society, Americans waste nine million hours per day searching for misplaced items.

The clutter quickly consumes our lives. Many books have been written about organizing your life. I list a few of my favorites in the bibliography in the back of this book. These books hit on many topics, but few venture into the need to organize your digital resources. This book will focus on organizing the digital resources that are cluttering your life both personally and professionally.

Students are also suffering from infoclutter. A research project can quickly immerse them into infoclutter. This overload can and often does turn into what I label "cut and paste" plagiarism. Plagiarism is easier than ever before since my early days of teaching. Back then, students at least had to handwrite what they copied, maybe changing a word or two. It even almost happened at my house.

PLAGIARISM AT HOME ■

To make a long story short, my seven-year-old almost plagiarized his first-grade animal research report. To make matters worse, I was sitting next to him while he was researching on the Internet! I caught this one; with the new skills you will learn, you can catch it too!

We settled into my home office ready to research the elusive Gila monster, and I was all ready to impart my knowledge when my seven-year-old put me in my place and asked Jeeves. Patrick promptly hyperlinked himself to facts about a Gila monster which included a nice picture. With Patrick on a safe Web site, I turned my attention to one of the many piles in front of me. Patrick checked out the information, reading little and clicking lots, and decided this would be a good Web site to use.

I noticed Patrick was clicking up in the menus looking for something, and I helped him locate the edit menu, select all, and then back up to copy. About now, I turned my full attention back to Patrick and watched him. Next, Patrick opened up the word processing program and asked me how to paste.

In an instant, it was all done, report and picture of the Gila monster! Print, sign your name, and on to build the habitat in the shoebox. Wow! Right in front of me on my computer a plagiarizer was created! Of course, I put a quick stop to that and tried to explain why it was wrong. Then, the teacher in me used Inspiration software to create a web filled with facts, and we created an original report. No shoebox habitat was built until the report was done!

Stories

INFOCLUTTER EVERYWHERE ■

Parents are also suffering from infoclutter. Information used to flow home just through the backpack. Now e-mail helps connect parents, teachers, and administrators. Web pages can be used for up-to-the-minute homework updates. In some cases, student lunches can be ordered on-line. Homework help can bring up millions of results, and which ones are valid anyway? The digital images posted on the class Web page bring a field trip home. One last thing, do not forget the backpack!

There is also administrative infoclutter. Once, the mailbox in the office was the mailbox to dread. Now, add on the untamed e-mail inbox available for deposit of e-mail anytime. Infoclutter has file cabinets overflowing along with servers. Administrators need specialized skills to reduce the clutter.

■ WHO SHOULD READ THIS BOOK?

This book was designed for all educators including those of us that were in the classroom before the computers were. In the information age, every teacher needs a digital foundation. The digital foundation developed throughout this book is what every teacher needs to be successful in the information age. This book is all about practical, simplified, real ways to manage the information flowing to you from various sources.

Read this book alone and make changes that will have you saving time today. Pull a small group together and support each other as you tackle various chapters. Professional developers may use this book with the entire staff to help everyone save time. For those of you involved in preservice education, use this book so those future teachers start teaching with a strong digital foundation. For those taking classes on-line, this is a perfect book easily adapted to an on-line course.

This book is filled with focus questions, preassessments, postassessments, and activities. Work together with a group on-line or at alone at home and start saving time today. Some of the sections included are detailed in the following chart.

■ TIMESAVING TIPS THROUGHOUT THE BOOK

Self-Assessments	These are located on the first few pages of each chapter. These can be used as a preassessment or points for discussion.
Stories and Examples	Look for the icons to identify stories and examples that illustrate the chapter elements.
Tryout Activities	These are flexible activities to be used individually or in small or large groups. Some have been designed for staff and some are for students.
Focus Questions	These focus questions can be discussion starters designed to help personalize this book for your specific needs.

Action Plan	Each chapter ends with an action plan to start using your new skills immediately. Timesaving skills must be practiced to become personal.
Professional Development Tips	Located throughout the book are tips and ideas for those using the book for professional development sessions.

From the "technophobic" to the Web master, there is something for everyone. There are some topics covered that the instructional technology (IT) staff may not personally need but are very helpful as they work with staff to help save time. Charts, screen shots, and stories are used to reach a variety of skills levels.

The term *timesaving* is used repeatedly throughout the book. Timesaving is so critical for every teacher. Conducting a search and looking through thousands of resources is frustrating and wastes the precious time we have. Tips, strategies, and solutions will be shared throughout. Refer to the companion Web site for new tips.

THE COMPANION WEB SITE ■

To accompany this book, I have created a companion Web site. The Web site can be found at http://www.infoclutter.com. This Web site will be updated regularly to keep the links active and the content fresh. All the links in this book will be hyperlinks on the Web site. Feel free to share the Web site and activities found on-line.

Timesaving ways to use the links in the book:

1. Visit the companion Web site located at http://www.infoclutter.com. The Web site will be updated regularly.

2. Type the address to check if the address is correct and the link does not work.

3. Search for the domain and see if you can navigate from there. For example, if the address is http://www.techteachers.com/math.htm, search for techteachers and see if you can find the page for which you are looking.

PROFESSIONAL DEVELOPMENT TIPS ■

In planning professional development experience, this book can be used in a variety of ways. If at all possible, try to create sessions for teachers where they can use the technology with which they are familiar and access the data files they would like to organize. This is a highly personal type of professional development with some staff members needing extensive support while others can help facilitate the group. Throughout the book, I will add tips that are appropriate for the topics. Check the companion Web site often for professional development updates.

The digital foundation is what timesaving technology is all about. Some of the skills include organizing and managing files in a digital filing cabinet, sharing information on the network, using e-mail to share information, locating information quickly on-line, and many other skills teachers need to have to feel comfortable using technology. These foundations must be in place to help teachers save time and make the most of technology.

Educators of all abilities need support. This is the starting point to developing a digital foundation on which teachers can build. Take a step back to examine the digital foundation and fill in the cracks; this will lead to a solid base for growing and developing great experiences.

Activity 1

Your Seven-Step Plan for
Personal Professional Development

1. Identify Roadblocks

Who in your life knows more about technology than you do?

What has been holding you back?

What are your technology fears?

2. Tech Support

Who can you turn to for some help at home and school?

What resources do you have to learn more?

What professional development may be available to you?

3. Tech Know-How Goals

What do you want to learn how to do?

What are you doing now that using technology could help save you time?

4. Start Simple

What is a simple project you could try to get started?

Brainstorm some other simple "get started" projects.

5. Add On

How can you expand that simple project?

What is another activity you could tackle with your new skills?

6. Push Yourself

Now that your simple project is done, what is your next project goal?

What new skills do you need to complete this project?

7. Celebrate

How will you celebrate your new skills?

With whom will you share your progress?

Copyright © 2004 by Corwin Press, Inc. All rights reserved. Reprinted from *Conquering Infoclutter: Timesaving Technology Solutions for Teachers* by Meghan Ormiston. Thousand Oaks, CA: Corwin Press, www.corwinpress.com. Reproduction authorized only for the local school site that has purchased this book.

Action Plan for Conquering InfoClutter

1. What topics do you want to learn more about?

   a.

   b.

   c.

   d.

2. Specifically, how can professional development activities be developed to support teachers?

3. What professional development do you need?

4. What digital foundations do you need to strengthen?

5. What are some of the benefits of using technology in the classroom?

Focus Questions for Conquering InfoClutter

1. Why is it important to make professional development personal?

2. What are digital foundations?

3. Why is it important for teachers to understand the benefits of using technology?

4. What does infoclutter look like in your life?

5. What are your first steps to tame the infoclutter?

Copyright © 2004 by Corwin Press, Inc. All rights reserved. Reprinted from *Conquering Infoclutter: Timesaving Technology Solutions for Teachers* by Meghan Ormiston. Thousand Oaks, CA: Corwin Press, www.corwinpress.com. Reproduction authorized only for the local school site that has purchased this book.

2

Sharing to Save Time

We teach the concept of sharing. As educators, sharing with peers can be very intimidating, and often teachers do not have the time needed. Technology tools provide new and exciting ways to share to help reduce the isolation many teachers experience. There are so many resources available to teachers that we need to give teachers permission to share, create new ways to share, and reward sharing in our schools. This chapter will showcase some of the ways teachers are sharing so that they are not reinventing the wheel each day.

Share through e-mail, on the network, on-line, in discussion groups, and with the teacher across the hall. Many teachers find it easier to share things anonymously with other staff members. Because it is risky to share, teachers need support and encouragement to start sharing resources. You will leave this section with practical ways to make this happen and save time.

Professional Development

I recently had the wonderful opportunity to visit a school district in the Southwest United States. In preparation for my keynote address, I researched what types of shared resources are available to teachers in the state. I used my advanced searching strategies you will soon have to locate one of the best collections I have ever seen.

I showed a number of wonderful resources off the Web site that is open not only to teachers in the state, but to everyone on-line. As I raved about how wonderful this collection was, how it was so well organized, and how it aligned to the state learning standards, I was surprised that so few teachers in the group used the Web site.

In following up with the surprised technology department afterward, they explained that they had been to every building during the year showing the collection and explaining how to access the resources. We discussed a new plan to get the word out and made a plan of action. One of my thoughts was that teachers had not been given an opportunity to explore the Web site on their own, locate what they needed, and store this away in their own digital filing cabinet.

All the resources in the world will not help teachers unless they have a chance to explore the resources and organize them in a way that makes sense to them. This section will look at on-line digital filing cabinets and other educators who are sharing resources. We will explore directories for teachers, students, and parents. We will also learn about WebQuests and collaborative projects. Specific strategies and stories from teachers are shared throughout the chapter.

Self-Assessment for Sharing to Save Time: Where Are You Now?

Self-Assessment

1. If you have a network at school, what is it used for?

2. How can you use e-mail to share resources?

3. In what ways can technology help your grade level, department, or team share resources?

4. What types of teaching resources are found on the Internet?

5. What makes sharing difficult in schools?

6. What is a WebQuest, and how can it be used?

7. How are primary source documents being used in schools?

8. How can you share resources outside the building?

Copyright © 2004 by Corwin Press, Inc. All rights reserved. Reprinted from *Conquering Infoclutter: Timesaving Technology Solutions for Teachers* by Meghan Ormiston. Thousand Oaks, CA: Corwin Press, www.corwinpress.com. Reproduction authorized only for the local school site that has purchased this book.

The reality of what is happening is that we are drowning in paper. This paper overload is a roadblock to making significant changes in the digital world. All the stacks of papers, piles, and files make up print infoclutter. Before tackling your digital transformation, let us explore the current realities.

■ ARE YOU PAPER-TRAINED?

The biggest roadblock to sharing information digitally is the fact that most teachers and the majority of administrators are paper-trained. We love paper; we collect paper. Paper is everywhere.

Stacks of paper can be found at home, at school, in the car, in the garage, and in the basement, we still go to conferences and collect piles of paper. Long after teachers leave the classroom they still hold on to their "stuff." Take a look at the size of some of the "school bags" each morning at the mailboxes.

Most educators as a collective unit love paper. We need to acknowledge this and then try and change our ways. In recent years, there have been many educators who have announced their retirement and then the negotiation begins. First, it starts out very nicely with "have a great retirement, relax, have fun, travel, sleep in," and so forth. This is quickly followed up by "can I have your file cabinet?"

So, You Have a File Cabinet

File cabinets in schools are a hot commodity. Recently, I was working in an elementary school that was going through renovation. This wonderful old building was getting a much needed face-lift and new classroom furniture. A decision was made that each teacher would be issued a brand new two-drawer file cabinet. Two drawers, are you crazy?

These teachers could not stop talking about this awful thing that was happening to them. As a teacher, I sympathized with the staff, but it did help me to see that most teachers need to work on organizing all of this "stuff."

Are You the Binder King or Queen?

Every building has at least one. Binders filled with "stuff." The file cabinet may not be the problem here, but paper is weighing you down.

My Binder Nightmare

I was completing a project with a school in New Jersey and raced to the airport for a flight back to Chicago. I had been out of town for the week, so I had a few things with me, mainly my "school bag." The first flight was delayed, pushed off from the gate, and returned to the gate. The airline was able to get me on another flight home, but of course, it was on the other side of the airport.

Running through the Newark airport with my luggage and school bag was no treat on Friday night. I made it to my seat as they closed the door, and I promised myself that I would never carry so much again.

It was the two binders in the school bag that almost did me in. Once I caught my breath, I looked through the binders and found that most of the carefully punched sheets were Web pages printed off the Internet. Never again! Right there on the airplane I made the plans for my first Web site to be filled with links instead of paper. The Web site has changed about fifty times, but never again will I run through the airport with copies of Web sites!

The organization chapter is filed with ways to deal with digital resources. My digital filing cabinet has helped me lighten my load as I share my resources with other teachers.

Stop the Printing

Stop hitting the print command. It happens to all of us; time is tight. We discover a great Web site, and we print now and read later.

Many teachers share resources with others by printing the Web site and putting it in the mailbox. The teacher thanks you for the Web site and then puts it in a file folder labeled "Web sites to look at." Sharing great Web site finds is wonderful, but save the trees and e-mail the link.

As networked computers begin to fill our schools, the use of paper actually increases. There is little possibility that we will ever experience a paperless school, but we need to create new systems to better manage the information we need.

With All the Files, Binders, and Boxes, Can You Find What You Need?

With the hundreds, if not thousands of pounds of paper, can you put your hands on what you need? Can you locate exactly what you need quickly? If the answer is yes, that is great! The paper may be under control, and now strategies for organizing digital resources are next. This book will help you make the most of your organizational skills as you create and organize your digital files and on-line resources.

If your answer is sometimes, we will give you very practical tips that you can start using today. If your answer is rarely, this is the place to start. This book will help you clean the slate and get started down the path of complete organization, and you will save time.

DIGITAL RESOURCES TO SHARE ■

You can create your own collection of Web site resources specific to your curriculum. This can be as simple as cutting and pasting addresses into a word processing document to making a complex Web site. In Chapter 6, step-by-step skills can be found. Before creating your own, we will explore the many resources other teachers have created.

Teachers are sharing great things on-line. This section looks at "general sites" for teachers. In Chapter 9, specific-content Web sites are detailed. To browse through teachers' resources, here are a few places to start.

■ LESSON PLAN DIRECTORIES

There are many initiatives, projects, and learning communities that share educational resources on-line. Teachers all over the globe have created excellent lesson plan collections. Many Web sites allow educators to search for materials, and some make it possible to add lessons to the collection.

Cyberguides

One of my favorite lesson plan collections was created in California. The on-line home is the Cyberguide project from teachers in California which can be found at

http://www.sdcoe.k12.ca.us/score/cyberguide.html

California teachers have created these supplemental literature-based units. Teachers all over the world tap into these resources filled with great resources and active links to on-line Web sites. The current K-3 page has over 42 units.

Cyberguides are supplementary, standards-based, Web-delivered units of instruction centered on core works of literature. Each cyberguide contains student and teacher editions, standards, a task and a process by which it may be completed, teacher-selected Web sites, and a rubric based on the California Language Arts Content Standards. In the cyberguides, the magenta text indicates the language (or context-appropriate equivalent to the language) of the content standards.

WebQuests On-line

Thousands and thousands of WebQuests have been created and published on-line by teachers. But what is a WebQuest?

A WebQuest is an inquiry-oriented activity in which most or all of the information used by learners is drawn from the Web. WebQuests are designed to use learners' time well, to focus on using information rather than looking for it, and to support learners' thinking at the levels of analysis, synthesis and evaluation. The model was developed in early 1995 at San Diego State University by Bernie Dodge with Tom March and was outlined then in Some Thoughts about WebQuests found at http://edweb. sdsu. edu/ courses/edtec596/about_webquests.html. The theoretical basis for WebQuests is Marzano's "Dimensions of Learning" Model.

Many WebQuests are developed with a hook or a real-life problem that starts the exploration. Standards are used in development of WebQuests and are usually listed in the teacher's notes.

There are many collections of WebQuests on-line, starting with the largest collection updated by Bernie Dodge. I always start with this collection because these are all true WebQuests, not scavenger hunts or "internetized" lessons called WebQuests. Each WebQuest is organized in the same way, helping teachers to focus on the content instead of organizational elements.

In addition to searching through the directories of WebQuests, one can search for specific WebQuests by using keywords. For example, if I wanted to search for a WebQuest about weather, I may go to a search engine and search using the keywords Webquest + weather + primary.

Other WebQuest collections can be found at:

Bernie Dodge's WebQuest collection: http://webquest.org/

My directory of WebQuests: http://www.techteachers.com/unittable. htm

Blue Web'n Web site links: http://www.kn.pacbell.com/cgi-bin/ searchApps.pl

Spartenburg's collection: http://www.spa3.k12.sc.us/WebQuests. html

Primary Source Lessons

Using primary source documents in a classroom helps students make real-life connections. Many document collections can now be found on-line. In the United States, many of the important historical documents can be found at the National Archives headquartered in Washington, D.C. In the Digital Classroom section of the Web site, teachers have selected primary source documents and created lessons around the documents. The National Archives shares these lessons on-line for everyone to use.

A collection of lesson plans utilizing primary source documents from the National Archives can be found at http://www.archives.gov/digital_ classroom/index.html

The Library of Congress is also filled with primary source documents and exciting resources for students and teachers. The collections are beautifully displayed and rich with information. One of the challenges is staying focused and on track while exploring the thousands of pages available.

Lesson ideas from the Library of Congress can be found at http://www.memory.loc.gov/ammem/ndlpedu/lessons/primary. html

And Now ....
A Word from Our Sponsor
A WebQuest about Persuasive Techniques

**Team 3 - Grade 8
Shepherd Middle School
Ottawa, Illinois**

Introduction | Process | Product | Resources | Evaluation | Standards | Credits

Figure 2.1   An example of a middle school WebQuest

At the state level, there may also be collections available to you for conducting research. One such collection is from Alabama. Depending on your location, the local historical society may have a collection of resources for you.

Alabama Achieves lessons that easily could be adapted can be found at http://www.archives.state.al.us/teacher/psources.html

Outside the United States, there are also thousands of collections available to explore. Using your advanced search skills, many of these collections may be indexed by search engines and open to explore.

Individual Teachers Sharing Great Things

A collection of lesson plans and handouts by Ray Saitz and other contributors, this Web site is filled with resources for language arts: http://home.cogeco.ca/~rayser3/

Frank Potter's Science Gems includes science collections for all grade levels: http://www.sciencegems.com

Mrs. Silverman's collection for the primary grades is filled with collaborative project ideas and cross-curricular lesson plans: http://www.kids-learn.org

More Lesson Plan Collections

Lesson collection Teachers Helping Teachers: http://www.pacificnet.net/~mandel

Lesson Bank: http://www.teachers.net/lessons

Lessons, activities, and worksheets available from Teachnet: http://www.teachnet.com/lesson/index.html

A to Z Teachers Stuff: http://www.atozteacherstuff.com/lessonplans

Los Angeles, California collection of Web resources: http://teams.lacoe.edu/documentation/places/lessons.html

SHARING ON THE SCHOOL ■ NETWORK TO SAVE TIME

The school network is a great timesaver; it can also be very confusing. Before going on, take a moment to draw a picture, write about, or explain to someone else how your school network is organized. Take a guess if you have no idea. This will help you better understand the next section.

Network 101 (Just the Basics)

Most school networks are set up in a similar way. Without getting technical, your network administrator sets up "rights" for each person who accesses the school network. Based on the "rights" assigned, the user will have specific permission to do certain things. For example, a student will not be able to access the teacher's files or shared teacher's files.

School networks are the perfect place to start sharing. Shared folders may be available right now. Within the shared folder, there can be subfolders for each grade level, group, or committee within the school. New folders may need to be added by the person responsible for the network.

Teacher Folder	This is your personal folder on the network.
Student Folders	Some schools have folders for student work.
Shared Folders	These folders share documents with a specific group (sometimes called the shared drive).

In most schools, teachers and students "log in" to the network. The username and password are the keys to getting to the things that have been assigned based on the "rights." Every network is set up in a different way. Navigating the network should be a workshop topic offered at every school.

Teachers need to understand how the network is organized and explore ways to use the network to save time. Many very talented classroom teachers struggle to understand the computer network and where things are saved. This is a very important building block to put in place for successful technology use.

Shared Folders Will Save You Time

The concept of shared folders is underutilized in most school systems. Administrators can use the shared folders to share information with the staff. In some systems, the daily or weekly updates are placed in a designated shared folder, and the staff is expected to retrieve the file. Some administrators share information with students using a shared folder open to all students and staff.

Sharing Reading Resources

I worked with a very talented first grade team over a number of sessions during the school year. My role was to support this group as they worked together to integrate technology. The time we spent on organization has saved countless hours.

Five first grade teachers in the same building came together and created a plan to share resources. This group worked with me to help create shared folders that they could all access on the network. We started with reading because this was the first year with a new reading book. We proceeded chapter by chapter, and as teachers had files they wanted to share on a given topic, they put it into the shared network file or the file folder if it was a "hard copy."

Lesson ideas, worksheets, activities, and Web sites were added to the units throughout the year. Now, in year two, planning has been simplified, and the real timesaving is under way. In team meetings, this group can reflect on what works and what still needs to be developed. Instead of each teacher reinventing the wheel, each teacher has access to the best resources from the team.

Two new team members added this year found the system to be a huge timesaver. Faced with a new curriculum, these file folders are an invaluable resource.

Spelling in New Ways

After we organized the reading units and filled them with content, we turned our attention to spelling. The spelling program also was new, and each teacher was planning to type the words each week. Each classroom is equipped with a large screen television mounted on the wall connected to the computer.

The first grade team split up the spelling words for the year and typed each list in a readable first grade font. Each Monday morning, the first grade teachers pull up the file and review the words with the class. The same files were modified (the font made smaller) and saved as the take-home list. Each teacher has the entire year of spelling organized and ready to use. The next time we would utilize parent volunteers to input the information.

The Middle School Gets Organized

For many years, the only resources teachers had were textbooks, support material that came with the textbook, and a few handwritten dittos to supplement what the textbook publisher bundled with that book. The textbook served as your curriculum, and you raced through it as fast as you could. In some ways, those days were easier.

Today, teachers face the challenge of aligning curriculum to state and local standards. This alignment is usually different from the textbook focus, and in many cases, you need to customize materials for your students. Teachers are generating more and more of their own materials and rarely are they handwritten any more.

A Dynamic Middle School Team Shares

This team of fifth grade teachers works in a middle school environment. This group had been working together for a number of years, and they worked very well as a team. Each teacher taught social studies, and most often the planning was done together.

During team meetings, this group would split up the tasks to complete for each social studies unit. For example, teacher A would recreate the textbook's test to better align to standards, Teacher B would create the review sheets, Teacher C would write out the presentation rubric, and Teacher D would pull together resources.

This went on for a number of years. Each teacher created the materials assigned and made hard copies for the others on the team. Each kept a file for the unit and pulled it out each year. The problem came when a change had to be made to one of the parts of the unit. Where was it saved?

Each teacher created the materials and saved them to the network under their own name. When someone else needed the copy, they had to have that person log on and hunt through the files. They had such a great system of sharing the work, and the network slowed them down instead of helping.

The solution was simple. We asked the network administrator to create a folder for this team. In the folder, we made subfolders for each unit. The team members went through their individual folders and saved them to the team folder. Now, when next year rolls around, everything is in one place and ready to go. This team now totally believes in shared folders, and almost everything goes there.

This was a great team to work with; they just needed a little network help. Most teachers do not know how or what to share on the network, which again adds to the isolation many teachers experience. This group was also lucky to have a large team with which to work.

Both the first grade and fifth grade teams probably had been sharing resources for many years. Hard copies have limits. When changes need to be made without the digital files, time is wasted retyping. When sharing files with your team, you give each member the ability to modify the document and personalize it to meet the needs of the students. As new teachers come to the school, the team resources can be shared to help save time for all.

As exciting as shared folders can be, it is important to understand that some things do not belong there. In most cases, each staff member has a personal folder. This is where teachers should save information about students or parental concerns. Understand your saving options to protect the data from unwanted access. When saving sensitive files, be particularly careful about saving to the appropriate folder by carefully selecting the "Save As" location.

Backing up the server is critical. Many networks are set to back up once per day. Your data on the server is backed up and "safer" than carrying floppies or on stand-alone computers that are not backed up. Backing up files is important.

Sharing Web sites is quick and easy using e-mail. Sending the link in an e-mail message will keep the link active. It is much easier to click on a Web site address link and see a Web site than it is to take the paper to the computer, type in the long and complicated Web site address, and hope it goes to the right place. Save time, and e-mail those great Web site discoveries.

Changing the way we share resources through e-mail or on the network will save each teacher time in locating resources and customizing them to meet individual needs. Get creative. Can you share resources with teachers from other schools in your district? Get together and plan how and what you will save and share. The power of the network is sharing; make it happen at your school.

Students Share Information

Many K-12 teachers are requesting student assignments be turned in digitally instead of on paper. Using the network, students can save assignments into a specified folder, and the teacher can get to the documents and make comments and corrections right in the document. Microsoft Office has some powerful features to insert comments without changing the student's work. This saves time as the teacher and students communicate digitally.

■ SHARE TO SAVE TIME

Reading about sharing is not going to save time, but action will. Take time to make this chapter personal by creating an action plan to improve the sharing of digital resources. Regardless of your technology skill level, understanding the concepts in the chapter will help. Take the time for reflection and planning by using the action plan and reflective questions.

Action Plan for Sharing to Save Time

1. Open and explore three lesson plan collections and record some thoughts on each Web site.

   a.

   b.

   c.

2. With the help of your network administrator, create a new shared folder and complete the following:

   a. Save a document into the new shared folder.

   b. Help another staff member open the shared folder.

   c. Help the other staff member save to this shared folder.

3. Meet with others teaching a similar subject and make an action plan to increase sharing to save time.

   a.

   b.

   c.

Copyright © 2004 by Corwin Press, Inc. All rights reserved. Reprinted from *Conquering Infoclutter: Timesaving Technology Solutions for Teachers* by Meghan Ormiston. Thousand Oaks, CA: Corwin Press, www.corwinpress.com. Reproduction authorized only for the local school site that has purchased this book.

Focus Questions for Sharing to Save Time

1. What is a cyberguide, and how can it be used?

2. How is a WebQuest different than a traditional lesson plan?

3. What are primary source documents, and how are they being shared on-line?

4. How can a team of teachers use the school network to save time?

5. What is a shared folder, and how can it be used?

6. How will you share in new ways?

Copyright © 2004 by Corwin Press, Inc. All rights reserved. Reprinted from *Conquering Infoclutter: Timesaving Technology Solutions for Teachers* by Meghan Ormiston. Thousand Oaks, CA: Corwin Press, www.corwinpress.com. Reproduction authorized only for the local school site that has purchased this book.

3

Speeding Up Internet Navigation: Timesaving Skills Everyone Needs

Searching and finding are two very different things when looking around the World Wide Web. This chapter focuses on improving searching skills. Of all the timesaving skills, this could save the most time. There is little time to waste in a teacher's day.

Starting in the right place is the first step. Selecting the correct resources includes looking beyond the Internet to print and multimedia materials. A quick search through the encyclopedia may be just what is needed to solve a quick question. The Internet is great, but along with looking at "how to" effectively search the Internet, we will look at how to validate the information found.

Professional Development

Internet literacy is the focus of this chapter. The Internet is organized differently than traditional print materials. Understanding how to navigate and evaluate will help streamline your next project. In many cases, the information you need is on-line, and this chapter will help you locate information more efficiently.

Information literacy training is best done with the entire staff and student population. Students often take what they find on-line as the absolute truth. Everyone needs to better understand the organization of the Internet.

Plagiarism is also a major problem in our schools at all levels. Cut-and-paste plagiarism is happening in early elementary school all the way through higher education. A section on plagiarism will help all educators have a better sense of how this is done. With a few tools from this chapter, you will be better prepared to detect plagiarism along with restructuring lessons so plagiarism is decreased.

Self-Assessment for Navigating the Internet: Where Are You Now?

Self-Assessment

1. List three challenges you face when using the Internet.

   a.

   b.

   c.

2. What search engine(s) are you currently using?

   a.

   b.

   c.

3. What skills would you like to learn?

   a.

   b.

   c.

4. What wastes time when using the Internet?

   a.

   b.

   c.

5. What other resources could be used instead of the Internet?

   a.

   b.

   c.

Copyright © 2004 by Corwin Press, Inc. All rights reserved. Reprinted from *Conquering Infoclutter: Timesaving Technology Solutions for Teachers* by Meghan Ormiston. Thousand Oaks, CA: Corwin Press, www.corwinpress.com. Reproduction authorized only for the local school site that has purchased this book.

■ THE INTERNET IS JUST ONE SOURCE

The Internet is a wonderful source for research and collecting information, but it is only one option. In many cases, the best way to save time is to open a book and quickly locate the information. The Internet is not for everything.

Do not forget about all the other resources around you, including:

- Books
- Maps and globes
- Videotapes
- Audiotapes
- Interviews
- Encyclopedias
- Archived materials
- Reference books

The library media specialist in the school is a great resource and can offer both staff and students an overview of the collection and help to select the best resource to save time. Before moving into more information about on-line tools, take some time to explore what is available in the school library, as well as the public library.

■ WHERE TO START THE SEARCH

Upon opening the Internet browser (usually Netscape or Internet Explorer), there are many Web sites where you can start the search process. Selecting the right starting point is the first step to saving time; before starting, have a clear focus on what you are looking for.

General Directories of Information

Internet directories are online collections of information that have been selected by people. Directories come in all shapes and sizes, from a small collection to very large collections of resources in various categories. A directory is a good place to browse through topics that are organized and grouped in various ways.

A directory often has a search feature. It is important to understand that you are only searching within the Web sites in the directory, not searching the entire Internet. You are limited in what you will find because the directories as well as the search engines cannot keep up with the thousands of Web pages added each day.

Let us take a look at some of the large directories. Yahoo is a directory that is not only the largest, but also the most used Internet directory. There are many additional services and personalization options. This is a general directory with much information on various topics.

Other Directories

The Open Directories Project: http://www.dmoz.org

The Encyclopedia Britannica: http://www.britannica.com

About.com guides help explore the directory: http://www.about.com

Directories for Teachers

In the ongoing quest to save time, directories are an organized way to browse on-line resources. A directory groups information into categories that can be searched or explored by browsing from link to link. Directories can be very helpful for teachers who are new to technology integration.

Kathy Schrock Leads the Way

Kathy Schrock was a pioneer in sharing resources with teachers. Kathy was a media center director on Cape Cod. Kathy was into the Internet long before the Internet was fun. Kathy collected and organized Internet resources as she discovered them. Soon Kathy was asked to share her resources with other teachers, and that was the start of the Kathy Schrock's Guide for Educators, now hosted by Discovery School.

Kathy could have kept her wonderful resources on her school network, but instead, she posted them to the Internet for all educators to use. This collection of resources has been screened by Kathy and is a great place to start your research.

Kathy now serves as a district technology administrator. Visit Kathy's directory at:

http://www.school.discovery.com/schrockguide/index.html

Kathy is a very organized and efficient person. Her work on Kathy Schrock's Guide for Educators has saved countless hours for teachers all over the world. Kathy has helped all of us cut through the infoclutter.

Education World

Education World has organized more than 500,000 Web site resources. These resources are all screened and organized and include units, activities, lesson plans, and thematic and seasonal lesson ideas. This Web site is updated daily, and the content is fresh and filled with rich activities. This Web site is specifically targeted to help teachers. The address for Education World is http://www.educationworld.com

Scholastic.com

Scholastic.com is now a free teacher Web site after many years of being a subscription Web site. The parent, teacher, and kid channels are also here and filled with lesson ideas and resources. All content areas are covered, but there is a strong language arts focus, often based on the Scholastic authors. The Web site address is http://www.scholastic.com

Discovery School

Kathy Schrock's Guide for Educators is just one piece of this large resource collection. Favorites include Puzzle Maker giving teachers the ability to create over ten different types of puzzles with vocabulary words or spelling words. From crossword puzzles to mazes, students of all ages will enjoy a change of pace. Discovery School's Web site is http://www.discoveryschool.com

The new clip art collection is also filled with great school related clip art. The clip art is royalty free and can be used on your Web sites, worksheets, or letters home. The animated collection is a perfect way to freshen up your Web page.

Education Planet

This collection for parents, students, and teachers indexes over 100,000 resources. The search even helps identify grade levels in the search results. By browsing categories or using search terms, finding information is quick and easy. This is one of the largest lesson plan collections on the Internet. The Education Planet Web site is http://www.educationplanet.com

Tools for new teachers are available for a reasonable annual fee. These tools include:

- Teachers Site Maker
- Newsletter Maker
- Learning Links
- Lesson Maker
- On-line Storage

The weekly e-mail newsletter is perfect for classroom teachers. Each week just the best links and resources are delivered to your e-mail inbox. Some resources will tie into seasonal events; others are focused on a content area. These newsletters cut through the infoclutter and deliver a small focused set of resources. These short little newsletters deliver fresh new ideas and strategies for integrating technology into the curriculum (see Figure 3.1 for example).

Tech Teachers

This is my directory for teachers. I created this Web site and directory to organize all my digital resources and share them with the world. My digital filing cabinet is located behind the resources link, and there you will find thousands of categorized and evaluated resources. Although my collection is smaller than Kathy Schrock's guide, the gems you find here will save you valuable time (see Figure 3.2).

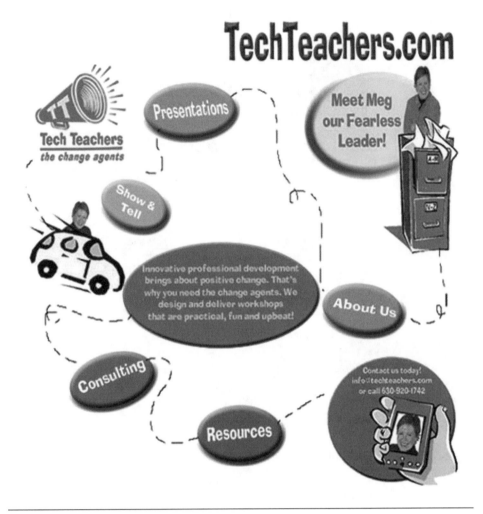

Figure 3.1   My website found on-line at http://www.techteachers.com

Directories for Students

Children need safe places to explore on the World Wide Web. Specific directories have been designed for students to help with research and to browse through topics. The content of these sites is filtered to help screen inappropriate Web sites. No filtering is perfect; so when students are on-line, keep an eye on where they are and what they are doing.

The three largest student directories are filtered versions of other popular adult directories. It is important to understand the differences before students start exploring. The adult directories are pictured on the left with the student version pictured on the right.

Basically, each of these sites has filtered the content to create a safer searching environment for kids. Although each of these sites has a search feature, you are only searching the Web sites that the Web site has organized into the directory. In other words, your search is limited to what the Web site has evaluated and indexed, and you may not find exactly what you are looking for.

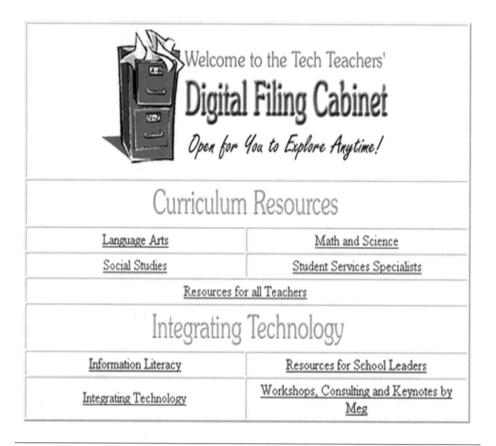

Figure 3.2   My digital filing cabinet

Ask Jeeves and Ask Jeeves Kids

Jeeves, what would we do without him? This is a natural language search engine, that is, you can put in questions instead of selecting key worlds. After typing a question, results are returned to you quickly.

Ask Jeeves is the unfiltered Web site (see Figure 3.3); Ask Jeeves Kids is the filtered Web site for students (see Figure 3.4). On the student Web site, there are a variety of other thematic resources and links for students to explore. I use this Web site all the time to try and answer the thousands of questions asked each day.

Yahoo and Yahooligans

Yahoo is the largest directory on the World Wide Web. Yahooligans is often used in elementary schools. Yahoo is filled with information ranging from news to travel. The Web directory is filled with resources on all topics. Yahoo can also be personalized with a number of features including the weather in your area, financial information, news, horoscopes, and layout.

The student directory is found on-line at http://www.yahooligans.com

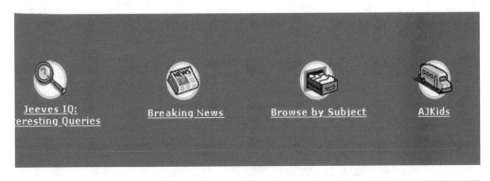

Figure 3.3   Ask Jeeves general site

This directory is filled with resources grouped for students. Searching the collection is an option, or one can just browse different topics. Most of the Web sites in the directory are easier for students to understand and use to collect information for research.

Student directories have been created to organize information and filter the content. Send the Web addresses home for parents to use. These directories have been created to organize information that has been evaluated. Although these Web sites are tested and checked often, we still need to supervise students as they use the Internet.

Directories for Parents

There are also directories that offer information to parents. These directories are filled with articles, activities, e-newsletters, chat rooms, and seasonal information. Some of the directories with helpful information for parents include:

Figure 3.4   Ask Jeeves for kids with filtered results

Family Education Network: http://www.familyeducation.com/home

National Parent Information Center: http://www.npin.org

Parents Place: http://www.parentsplace.com

Tech Teachers resources: http://www.techteachers.com/family_links. htm

Search Engines

Directories are great if you want to browse and explore a topic. If you know specifically what you are looking for, a search engine is where to start. There are a variety of types of search engines. Understanding the special functions and features of each type will save time. They include:

- Meta-search engines
- Specialized search engines
- General search engines

What Are "Meta-Search" Engines?

Meta-search engines search several search engines at the same time. This may sound good. Is it a good timesaving plan? No, meta-search is not what it used to be. Meta-searching is not one of the recommended strategies to save time. Let me explain.

What Is Wrong With Meta-Searching?

Meta-search engines do not own their own database of Web sites. Currently, none of the meta-search engines search Google (http://www.Google.com). In addition, many of the Web sites found when searching are not quality Web sites and often are filled with advertising. There have been a few changes recently as some of the Web sites have moved to a subscription service. Things may improve in the future. Meta-search engines include:

Search.com: http://www.search.com

DogPile: http://www.dogpile.com/index.gsp

IX Quick: http://www.ixquick.com

Specialized Search Engines

There are thousands of search engines on the Web, specializing in everything from pet name search engines to image search engines. A specialized search engine may save time and get to the information quickly. Before exploring the chart, find out about our discovery.

Very Specific Search Engines

I often work with small groups of teachers creating, planning, and preparing technology-rich lessons. On one such day, I was working with a fourth grade team going through a presentation on effective searching. Just before lunch, we were exploring the many specialized search engines teachers may use. As the teachers left for lunch, one of the teachers shared that she had a new kitten and just could not come up with a name.

The teachers headed out to lunch, and I stayed at the computer to work. I thought I would find some Web sites that may help the teacher name her cat. I was amazed at what I found by completing a simple search using the terms "cat names search engine." There on the screen were a number of search engines specializing in cats. Dogs were also equally represented.

Expand this idea to baby name search engines and get ready to look through hundreds of links. When the teachers returned from lunch, we spent a few minutes exploring the various search engines. With a few laughs, it became clear there were search engines for just about everything.

There are many collections to explore that will help you locate a specific search engine. In most of my searching, I use the advanced search features of Google to find what I need. If this does not work for what I am searching for, I then turn to a specialized search engine. A few collections to explore include:

Bernie Dodge's Collection of Specialized Search Engines: http://webquest.sdsu.edu/searching/specialized.html

Specialized search engines by Robert Harris: http://www.virtualsalt.com/search.htm

Select a Search Engine and Stick With It

If you use a different search engine every time you search, it is like going to a different grocery store every time you shop. Sure, you may find what you need, but it may just take you longer.

We have explored directories, meta-search engines, and specialized search engines, and now we are ready to explore a general search engine. Some search engines you may be using currently include:

Alta Vista: www.altavista.com

Google: www.Google.com

Lycos: www.lycos.com

Microsoft Network: www.msn.com

It does not matter what search engine you use. Use whichever search engine you are comfortable with, but learn how the search engine organizes the information. Each search engine does things a little differently. You may be able to find what you are searching for; it may just take more time.

Further Help With Searching

Becoming an effective searcher will save an enormous amount of time. There are a number of general tutorials available on-line. In most cases, each individual search Web site also has tips and strategies to make the best use of the features of the search engine. The following Web sites are filled with resources to help you become a more effective searcher:

Findspot.com is filled with tutorials and can be found at http://www.findspot.com

The largest collection of tutorials and guides for effective searching can be found at http://www.searchenginewatch.com

Noodle tools, a site filled with resources for teachers, can be located at http://www.noodletools.com

Activity 1

Searching Plan to Save Time

Plan what you are looking for.

1. What do you hope to find when you search?

   a.

   b.

   c.

2. Where should I start?

   a. Directory (If so, which one?)

   b. Meta-search engine (If so, which one?)

   c. Specialized search engines (If so, which one?)

   d. Search engine (If so, which one?)

3. What are some keywords related to the topic?

   a.

   b.

   c.

   d.

4. Are there any exact phrases that would help narrow the search (book titles or a person's name)?

5. Understanding the differences between directories and search engines, how will this save time and cut through the infoclutter as you use the Internet?

Copyright © 2004 by Corwin Press, Inc. All rights reserved. Reprinted from *Conquering Infoclutter: Timesaving Technology Solutions for Teachers* by Meghan Ormiston. Thousand Oaks, CA: Corwin Press, www.corwinpress.com. Reproduction authorized only for the local school site that has purchased this book.

Google to Save Time

Google is the search engine of choice for millions of people. Google works for me since it is fast, well organized, finds what I am looking for, and is neat and clean. The "clean" part sounds strange, but a side-by-side comparison illustrates this point. If I am on-line to search, I do not need to be distracted by all the other links.

The next section will take you through effective searching in Google. If it is possible to be on-line as you go through this section, try out your new skills. Most of the information in this section was adapted from the Google Web site. More help and information can be found on Google's site at

http://www.Google.com/help/refinesearch.html

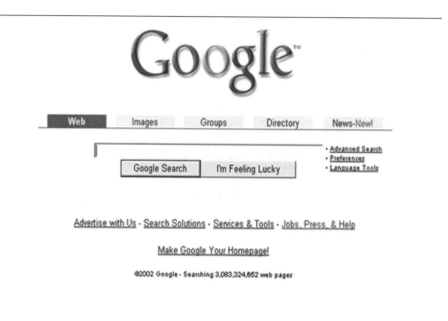

Figure 3.5   Google homepage

Activity 2

General Search Activity in Google

1. Select a very broad search term related to a curriculum topic (for example, space, reading, math, or weather).

2. Type this general term into the search box at www.Google.com. Click the Google Search button and record the number of results returned. This button is found in the upper right-hand corner on the blue bar. Number _____

3. Below the blue bar, there may be a directory line as well as news. Your first entry is titled and underlined. The Web address is listed in green below the description. Record the Web address here.

4. How many entries of the first ten may be helpful?

Copyright © 2004 by Corwin Press, Inc. All rights reserved. Reprinted from *Conquering Infoclutter: Timesaving Technology Solutions for Teachers* by Meghan Ormiston. Thousand Oaks, CA: Corwin Press, www.corwinpress.com. Reproduction authorized only for the local school site that has purchased this book.

■ ADVANCED SEARCHING SKILLS

A general search can be a big waste of time. No one has time to search through hundreds of thousands of Web sites. No more general searches here or in any search engine. It is time to learn advanced searching time-saving strategies. To begin with, click on the Advanced Search link on the Google homepage. A form appears with boxes to fill in.

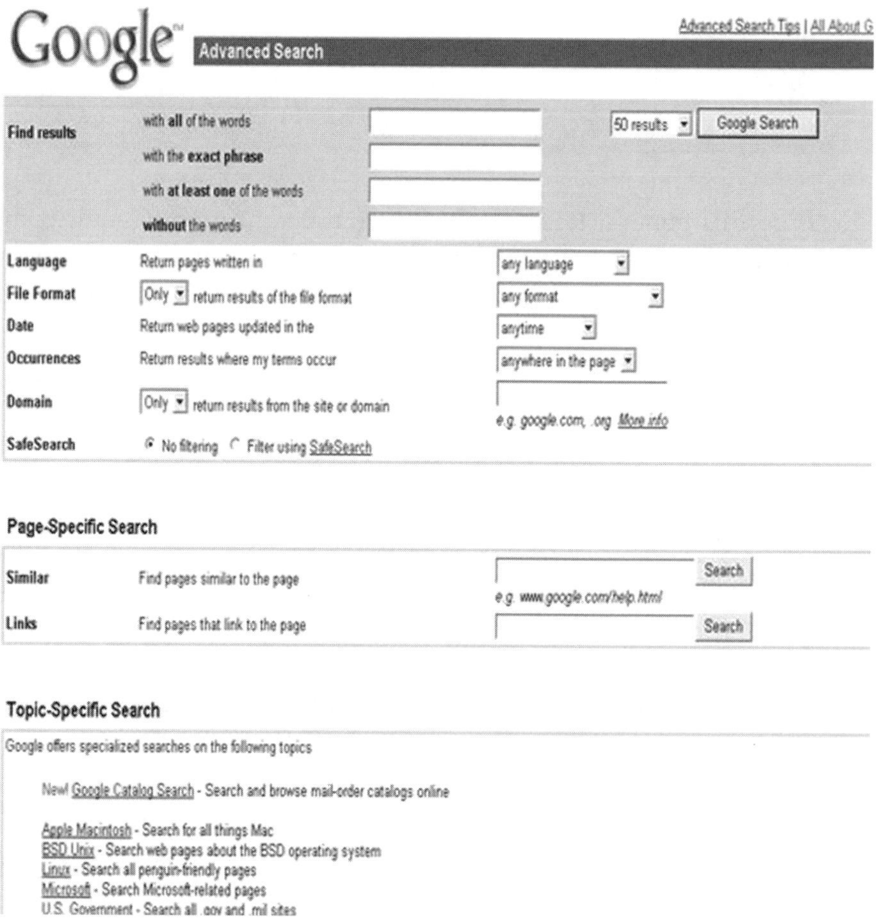

Figure 3.6   The advanced search page in Google

Keywords

Good keywords can get you exactly what you are looking for. Be specific. If you teach primary grades, use primary as a keyword. If you would like a WebQuest, use that as a term. Any word that focuses your search will help bring down the number of results and help you get exactly what you are looking for. The terms will be searched in the order in which you type them. Put the most important keywords first.

These keywords are typed in the first box in the form labeled "with all of the words." List the words with a space between each. Hit enter and record how may results you now have. Skip little words such as "and, the," since Google eliminates those words if they are listed as keywords. Forget about proper capitalization. Capital letters or small letters, Google searches the same way.

Google does not use word-stemming. In other words, if you type in WebQuest, Google searches WebQuest not WebQuests. For best results, try both versions of the word such as WebQuest and WebQuests.

Exact Phrase Searching

The exact phrase box is one of the biggest timesavers and the best way to accurately get results. After you enter an exact phrase in the box, Google will search for that phrase by keeping all of the words in the exact order that you typed them. This is a perfect way to search for a title of a book, song, famous quote, or anything that appears as a phrase.

Type in a title of a book in the exact phrase box and see how many results are returned. After checking the number, add a few keywords like cyberguide, WebQuest, and lesson plan to the top box and check the number of results.

The exact phrase feature is a great way to locate a specific string of words. For example, you may only remember a few words of a poem or song. Type in what you remember, and the search engine will search for the complete text. I often use this when I can remember a short phrase or quote and want to get back to the complete document.

Your Personal Google Activity

Your activity is to "Google yourself" using keywords if needed to narrow the search. How many results did your name get? Check out a family or friend.

With at Least One of the Words Box

The "with at least one of the words" box will retrieve pages with either word A or B. Use an uppercase "OR" between the keywords; for example, a search on measurement in either Math OR Science. Any of the boxes can hold information, but it is important not to repeat words. For example, if you have used "lesson plan" as a keyword do not add it to the "with at least one of the words" box as lesson OR WebQuest. Many teachers planning interdisciplinary units use this feature to check for results across various content areas.

Without the Words Box

Another way to eliminate some of your search results would be to select terms that you do not want included. For example, if your searches are returning results from higher education, eliminate them by typing the words in the "without the words" box. Any of these boxes can be changed after viewing the results. Try and test each box and see what happens to the search results. As you explore other search engines, you will find similar features.

Other Advanced Search Features

- *Language:* Foreign language teachers or bilingual teachers should check out this option on the advanced search page. Currently, you can select from 35 different languages in which to complete a search.
- *Date:* If you know when the information was placed on the Web page, select date. This is helpful if you are searching for current events or recent documents and reports.
- *Occurrences:* Where do you expect the terms selected to appear? Anywhere on the page, in the title, or in the Web address?
- *Domains:* This is used if you know the Web site you want to search. If you know that what you are looking for is on the NASA site, use this feature.
- *Safe Search:* Google's Safe Search filters some things, but continues to monitor the students while they are surfing.

The Google Image Search

If you need a picture or some clip art, head to Google. Using the same search strategies used to find Web sites, enter your advanced search but on the tabs across the top click on the Images tab. Over 400 million images are indexed. Some of these images may be copyrighted; follow the link to the Web site to collect information on use restrictions.

The Google Toolbar

I have the timesaving Google toolbar in front of me all the time. I quickly type a term in the box, and it searches directly from whatever Internet site I am viewing at the time. This little addition is free, easy to install, and absolutely a huge timesaver. For more information about the Google toolbar, check Google's homepage or go directly to this link:

http://www.toolbar.Google.com

At the time of print, the Google toolbar is only available for Windows machines running Internet Explorer.

Other Timesaving Tools from Google

Google has specialized search engines ready for you to use. These can be found at http://www.Google.com/options/specialsearches.html

These include United States government search, Linux search, Apple Macintosh search, and Microsoft search. New, specialized search engines are added to Google on a regular basis. These range from catalog shopping search engines to the Google news search engine. The ever-changing resources can be found at http://www.Google.com/options/index.html

Activity 3

Independent Advanced Google Search

Advanced searching is the way to save time. Select a new topic and complete the following questions. Your goal is to see how quickly you can narrow your search to fewer than 10 relevant results.

1. What is your main topic?

2. List some keywords about the topic.

   a.

   b.

   c.

3. Is there an exact phrase you are looking for, and what is the exact phrase?

4. What would you like to find (WebQuests, lesson plans, or reading guide)?

5. How many Web sites did you get?

6. How can this be refined?

7. How relevant are the results?

8. What new timesaving skills did you learn?

Copyright © 2004 by Corwin Press, Inc. All rights reserved. Reprinted from *Conquering Infoclutter: Timesaving Technology Solutions for Teachers* by Meghan Ormiston. Thousand Oaks, CA: Corwin Press, www.corwinpress.com. Reproduction authorized only for the local school site that has purchased this book.

■ PLAGIARISM IN AN INFOCLUTTERED WORLD

No one likes to talk about plagiarism, but it is a big problem in our K-12 classrooms as well as for higher education. After locating information on the Internet, students use the quick cut, copy, and paste functions of a word processing program to produce a document. Some students will leave it as is, add their name to someone else's work, print, and turn it in.

More sophisticated students will change the fonts, layout, and a few words here or there. All students need to know and understand that this is wrong. Many students admit to cheating but think their teachers will never figure out from where the information came. Insist on full documentation of resources and modify and change assignments each semester or school year.

Learn a few plagiarism detection skills and use them to let students know the work is being checked.

Plagiarism Detection

A well-informed instructor is the best defense against students turning in documents that have been plagiarized. There are a number of Web sites and tutorials found on-line.

Plagiarized.com is a Web site designed for instructors to learn more about plagiarism. The many activities will help instructors modify lessons to make them more difficult to plagiarize.

An on-line plagiarism tutorial for teachers is located at http://www.lemoyne.edu/library/plagiarism.htm

Plagiarism needs to be talked about with staff and students, and detection and prevention should be part of every professional development plan. Each school should use the many resources to set expectations, guidelines, and consequences that are consistent from department to department.

Google as a Detection Tool

If a paper comes across the desk that sounds suspicious, a powerful detection tool is the exact phrase search in Google's "Advanced Search." In the advanced search, type in the suspect sentence and see if you link back to one of the Web sites the students used. In many cases, showing your new skills to the class will dramatically reduce the number of students attempting to cut, copy, paste, and make it their own.

The following student research guide was created for a middle school to help students and teachers plan the research process and hopefully decrease the cut, copy, and paste plagiarism.

Activity 4

Research and Assignment Organizer and Guide

Name

Today's date

Class

1. What is your task? What is your topic?

2. What questions will help you find out more information about the topic?

    a.

    b.

    c.

    d.

3. Where will you search for information about the topic?

Copyright © 2004 by Corwin Press, Inc. All rights reserved. Reprinted from *Conquering Infoclutter: Timesaving Technology Solutions for Teachers* by Meghan Ormiston. Thousand Oaks, CA: Corwin Press, www.corwinpress.com. Reproduction authorized only for the local school site that has purchased this book.

4. What keywords or concepts will you look up?

   a.

   b.

   c.

   d.

5. How will you limit your research?

6. How will you check the information is valid?

7. How will you record the information as you find it?

8. How will you communicate or present the results?

9. When is this assignment due?

Copyright © 2004 by Corwin Press, Inc. All rights reserved. Reprinted from *Conquering Infoclutter: Timesaving Technology Solutions for Teachers* by Meghan Ormiston. Thousand Oaks, CA: Corwin Press, www.corwinpress.com. Reproduction authorized only for the local school site that has purchased this book.

One Higher Education Solution

While researching this section, I came across a Web site designed to help teachers detect plagiarism, which can be found at http://www.turnitin.com

Some of the features of this Web-based product include:

- Students submit their papers to the Web site before they are turned in to the teacher.
- The papers are then compared against a database of existing term papers.
- Within 24 hours, the teacher receives a report that details anything suspicious in the paper.
- This subscription service is available at many universities and high schools.

MAKE A PLAN TO BECOME A ■ BETTER NAVIGATOR OF THE INTERNET

This section scratched the surface about all the timesaving ways to conquer infoclutter. More timesaving tips will be covered throughout the rest of the book. Your new searching skills are one of the best things you can do to save time. Practice these skills by searching often. Practice to save time.

Action Plan for Navigating the Internet

1. List three challenges you face when you use the Internet.

   a. _____

   b. _____

   c. _____

2. What is one new skill you will put into action?

3. Why use a directory?

4. List a directory for:

   a. Teachers

   b. Students

   c. Parents

5. What is a meta-search engine?

6. List two reasons to use Google as your search engine.

   a. _____

   b. _____

7. What should you add to your browser to speed up searching?

Copyright © 2004 by Corwin Press, Inc. All rights reserved. Reprinted from *Conquering Infoclutter: Timesaving Technology Solutions for Teachers* by Meghan Ormiston. Thousand Oaks, CA: Corwin Press, www.corwinpress.com. Reproduction authorized only for the local school site that has purchased this book.

Focus Questions for Navigating the Internet

1. What is a directory?

2. What teacher-specific directory will you spend more time exploring?

3. What is the difference between a directory and a search engine?

4. What directories are safer for K-8 students to use for research?

5. What is wrong with meta-searching?

6. Which search engine do you plan on using and why?

7. Where can you go to find out more information about search engines?

Copyright © 2004 by Corwin Press, Inc. All rights reserved. Reprinted from *Conquering Infoclutter: Timesaving Technology Solutions for Teachers* by Meghan Ormiston. Thousand Oaks, CA: Corwin Press, www.corwinpress.com. Reproduction authorized only for the local school site that has purchased this book.

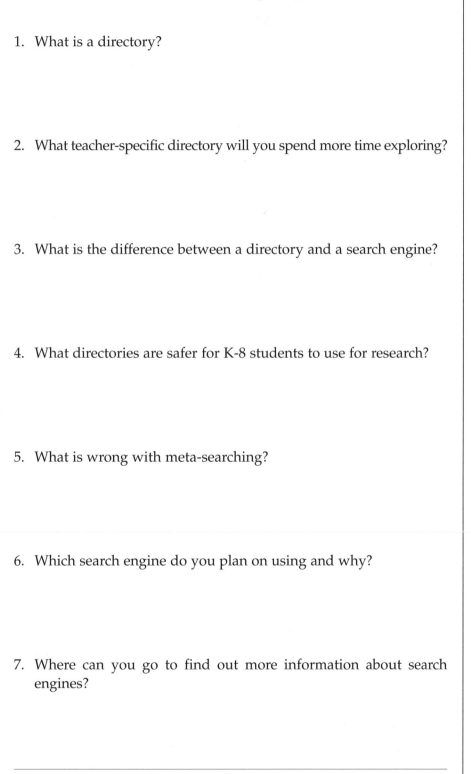

Focus Questions

4

Organizing to Conquer the InfoClutter

This organization chapter is the cornerstone—the foundation of timesaving. Hundreds of hours are lost each year looking for documents and files. This chapter is designed to cover the practical skills you need to organize your data files so that you can find things once they have been saved. Specific timesaving strategies will be provided in each section.

Everyone organizes information in a unique way. Some systems definitely work better than others. Binders, color-coded file cabinets, or rolodexes are paper-based systems that are designed to save time. Taking the basics of the paper-based system, a new system will be created for your digital files. Organization is the key to saving time.

Files are everywhere. Some are on disk, some are on the network, some are at home, some are on CD-ROMs, and some are on removable storage disks. With all this data everywhere, where do you start?

If this describes a system you know, help is here. The nuts and bolts of organizing files are rarely part of professional development, and with each file created, the problem is compounded.

Professional Development

Self-
Assessment

Self-Assessment for Organizing
to Save Time: Where Are You Now?

1. How are your documents filed right now?

2. What problems have you had locating files you have saved previously?

3. What would you like to change about your organizational system?

4. How do you back up your data?

5. What challenges do you face when sharing data between home and school?

6. What are your organization goals?

Copyright © 2004 by Corwin Press, Inc. All rights reserved. Reprinted from *Conquering Infoclutter: Timesaving Technology Solutions for Teachers* by Meghan Ormiston. Thousand Oaks, CA: Corwin Press, www.corwinpress.com. Reproduction authorized only for the local school site that has purchased this book.

Most educators need help in the file management area. Without specific systemic formal training, many people have stumbled along and created some sort of system. The biggest waste of time is when you go to retrieve something from the "system" or in most cases, the "digital dumping ground" known as "My Documents."

Designing the system will be accomplished by following along through this chapter. Later, your old data files will need to be added to the new system. This time investment will pay off each time you go to pull up a document and it is found in the place you designed for it.

A system must be set up. A new or old system that works is the foundation of conquering infoclutter. You are ready to begin creating your "Digital Filing Cabinet."

ORGANIZING YOUR DATA FILES ■

Start with your paper-based organization system. Which of the following best describes you?

    A. File cabinet user
    B. Binder user
    C. Piles drive the organization
    D. System, what system?

The answers to the preceding pop quiz will help you look at the paper organization system. Every system is slightly different and managed in a different way. Whatever system you use for paper will help you better understand how your digital files need to be organized.

Designing Your Digital Filing Cabinet

When cleaning up any mess, it is easier to put things away if you have a place to put them. Along this journey to create a digital filing cabinet, trash will be "recycled," new folders will be created, everything will have a label that makes sense, and your system will be simplified to save you time.

We will use a file cabinet metaphor to explore and create the digital filing cabinet. If your file cabinet is stuffed full of documents and folders, finding things will be difficult. Make a plan to make your filing system easy to use.

For all computer users, either Macintosh or PC, there are two basic types of items that need to be filed. A folder is an object that can hold multiple folders, documents, or files. On the monitor screen, the icon for a folder looks like a mini file folder. Next, you have files or documents that usually have a small picture or icon next to the name used to save the file.

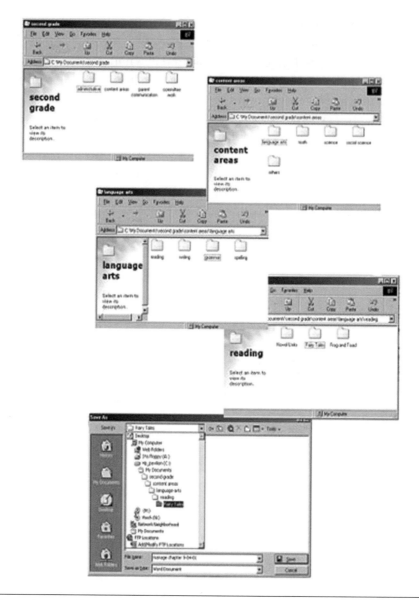

Figure 4.1   Files inside folders, in the new digital filing cabinet

Create Your Own Digital Filing Cabinet

It is time to start creating the main folders; think of these as your "digital file drawers." These are the four to five large folders; subfolders will be added next. This is a personal file system, so each set of four or five may be different. For right now, think of the big categories. Some examples may include:

- Content areas
- Administration
- Extracurricular
- Committees
- Mathematics
- Language Arts

Activity 1

Planning Guide for Your "Digital File Drawers"

1.

2.

3.

4.

5.

Stop at four or five; subfolders will be added.

Creating Your "Digital File Drawers"

These folders now become the four or five "digital file drawers" in your new digital filing cabinet. Move to the computer and on the desktop, look for an icon or label for documents. It may be called "My Documents," documents, or files, or it may be a simple file folder icon. By double-clicking your curser on this icon, it should open to reveal premade folders and possibly all the other files you have created in the past. Imagine all those individual files are in a pile on your desk just waiting to be filed into your new digital filing cabinet. If you do not see all of your past documents, they may be saved somewhere else, and once you create this new digital filing cabinet, you are ready to organize everything.

To create the first of your four or five folders, click on the File menu in the upper left corner, next select New, and then select Folder. A new folder appears in the window with the label new folder. Type the title of your first folder right over the highlighted text. You have created the first "digital file drawer" in your digital filing cabinet. Now repeat these steps with your remaining three or four labels.

Timesaving Tip

For PC users, a shortcut to creating folders is to click on the right button of the mouse, and the same File menu appears. Select New and continue on with the process. The right button on the mouse brings up various menus depending on what you are doing on the desktop or in a program. Just another one of those timesaving tips we all need.

Ready for Your "Digital Hanging Folders" or Folders Within Folders

You have your "digital file drawers" labeled, and now we proceed to "digital hanging folders." Next, we will get to the "digital file folders." Open your first "digital file drawer" by double-clicking your mouse. With an empty drawer, think about "digital hanging folders," some of the big ideas under your selected headings. Here think big ideas. Next, we will create subfolders. For example, if your first big drawer is content areas, now your "digital hanging folders" may be mathematics, language arts, social science, and science.

Activity 2

My "Digital Hanging Folders" Planning Guide

Plan before you start. Again, think big ideas under this topic.

1. The label on my "digital file drawer" is _____ .

2. Some of the big ideas for the "digital hanging folders" are:

Following the same plan for creating your "digital file drawers," you are ready to create "digital hanging folders." Click on the File menu in the upper left corner, next select New, and then select Folder. A new folder appears in the window with the label new folder. Type the title of your first folder right over the highlighted text. Repeat to complete your "digital hanging folders."

Your Own Digital Filing Cabinet in Three Quick Steps!

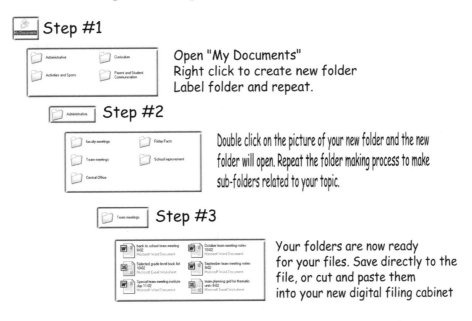

Step #1

Open "My Documents"
Right click to create new folder
Label folder and repeat.

Step #2

Double click on the picture of your new folder and the new folder will open. Repeat the folder making process to make sub-folders related to your topic.

Step #3

Your folders are now ready for your files. Save directly to the file, or cut and paste them into your new digital filing cabinet

Figure 4.2   Step by step through creating folders for the digital filing cabinet

---

Activity 3

My "Digital File Folders" Planning Guide

Plan before you start. Again think big ideas under this topic.

1. The label on my "digital hanging folder" is _____ .

2. Some of the big ideas for the "digital file folders" are:

Now the "Digital File Folders"

Open one of your newly created "digital hanging folders." Use the topics from your planning guide to create folders. In any of these steps you can always add folders in the future, so add a few to get started. Following the preceding example, your "digital hanging folder" language arts may now need subfolders that may include reading, writing, spelling, grammar, and so forth.

If You Are Ready, "Digital Subfolders"

Depending on the number of documents you have and personal preference, you can also create "digital subfolders." These would be folders within the "digital file folders." Depending on your needs, this will make you even more organized. Select any of the "digital file folders" and create new folders. Following the example in reading, your new folders may now include novel studies, reading strategies, assessments, related resources, and differentiation.

For Some of You, the "Digital Sub-Subfolder"

I personally am a big fan of sub, subfolders and have many on my hard drive. Finishing up the example in the "digital subfile folder," under novel studies I would have a folder for each novel we covered, where every worksheet assessment and activity would be filed. Next year everything is in one place ready to be shared with others. This process can go on and on.

Try it Out Activity!

Activity 4

Test Drive Your New Digital Filing Cabinet

Your new organization system is ready for a test drive.

1. Open your word processing program and under File select "Save As."

2. In the dialog box that pops up, label your file "test file 6–03."

3. Before hitting save, in the upper left-hand corner find the box labeled "Save in."

4. Click on the arrow to the right of the box and click on "My Documents."

5. Next, select one of your four or five folders.

6. Next, open a subfolder to put this new file into and click "Save."

7. You have added your very first file to your digital file cabinet. You can leave the file there or delete the file. Deleting files is covered in detail in the next section.

CONQUERING YOUR ■
DIGITAL DUMPING GROUND

You have systematically created your shiny new Digital Filing Cabinet, you have test driven it, and now it is time to put it to work. It is time to tackle your personal "Digital Dumping Ground." Before we start opening old files and floppies, new skills are needed to keep everything in order. Some of those new skills include naming files consistently.

Naming Files

Long ago when computers first made it into classrooms, the hard drive was very small, and there were not very many places for files to hide. As the hard drive space increases, so do the hiding places for your important data files. New strategies are needed to save time when you go to search for a file. The most important thing to remember is to be consistent.

Back in the days of DOS, PC users were limited to the number of characters used while saving a document. Now, the PC has caught up to the Mac world on this point, and you can now use up to 215 characters when you label a file or folder. Be careful here. There may be problems with big file names; stick to about 20 to 30 characters. Make the file name something you will understand in the future.

Dating everything is a huge timesaving step. Right after the file name, insert the date. Be careful to use a dash instead of a slash as you enter the date (7–03 instead of 7/03). Other characters you should not use when labeling files or folders are \, /, :, *, ?, ", <, >, and |. Even if you forget to file a document away, the date will help you select the appropriate document to repurpose. Putting the date first in the file name will by default organize all your files by date. Select the format that works for you (2–04 field museum permission or field museum permission 2–04). Pick a system that works for you and stick to it.

Bad File Names	Improved File Names
Letter home	First day of school letter to parents 8–03
Committee report	Math committee grade level report 11–03
Field trip	Field Museum field trip 2–04

Deleting Files

Your digital filing cabinet is ready to go, and it is time to take a hard look at the files you have collected. Nestled among your original files, you may uncover some files that you do not need anymore. It is time to pitch the junk you do not need and file away the good stuff in your new folders.

Before attacking your data files, let us delete the file you created to test out your new file cabinet:

1. Start by opening your new digital filing cabinet.

2. Double-click on the folder you saved the file in.

3. When you reach the file to delete, click on the file once, and then you can drag it to the Recycle Bin on the desktop. PC users can also hold the curser over the file and click on the right button on the mouse. By right-clicking, a menu appears with one of the options as "Delete."

4. Select "Delete," and your file is sent to the Recycle Bin.

If you make a mistake, do not panic; your file is not gone yet. Anything can be removed from the Recycle Bin before it is emptied. The file you deleted is empty, so we are safe to empty the Recycle Bin. PC users can right click and select "Empty the Recycle Bin"; Mac users can double-click on the trash and select "Empty trash."

Permission to File and Pitch

Now, it is time to roll up your sleeves and get to work. Depending on the number of files you have, clean up may take you awhile. You have permission to throw it away; do not file it if you would never use it again. Start by opening your old data storage system and taking a good look around. Make an attack plan and do not forget the drawer filled with floppies waiting to be filed.

Your digital filing cabinet is your new organization system; you now have a place for everything. Folders may need to be added as you start to work with your data. This is no problem. Make a new folder under your four or five lead folders. If you can tell what the file is from the label, you can quickly drag and drop it into the newly created folders. For those files that need to be open and examined, rename them with a new "Save As" name and date before filing or right click on a PC and rename. On a Mac click once on the file label and rename.

Some of the files you will uncover may not be needed anymore. By deleting these files, you free up space on your computer and simplify your life next time you search for a document. Depending on how old the files are, there is another option to make a folder labeled archives and file the old files here.

Celebrate

You have done a big portion of the hard work, and it is time to celebrate your accomplishment. You are on your way to a more organized digital life.

Activity 5

Digital Filing Cabinet Reflection Activity

1. What did you select for your four or five big ideas?

2. Once you had selected these, what subfolders have you created?

3. What sub-subfolders or files have you created?

4. What problems have you experienced in the past in file organization?

5. What files do you need to share with other teachers?

6. What can you throw away?

Copyright © 2004 by Corwin Press, Inc. All rights reserved. Reprinted from *Conquering Infoclutter: Timesaving Technology Solutions for Teachers* by Meghan Ormiston. Thousand Oaks, CA: Corwin Press, www.corwinpress.com. Reproduction authorized only for the local school site that has purchased this book.

■ REPURPOSING DOCUMENTS

One of the main reasons we went through the digital file cabinet organization was to create a system which you can easily navigate when you are looking for something. Real timesaving occurs when you reach into your file cabinet, dust off a document, repurpose the document, and use it again.

At the elementary level, a good example would be the welcome back to school letter sent home by many teachers. Each year this letter is basically about the same. Thinking like the timesaver that you now are, how could the letter sent home last year be repurposed?

Recently, I was asked to present a keynote address to a back to school institute day for elementary teachers. The session was going great, and teachers where soaking up new ways to save time when I started the repurposing section. This is the moment where many teachers could see the value in all this timesaving discussion.

I started by asking the teachers how many send home a welcome back to school letter. The majority of the group raised their hands. My next question was how many of you repurposed last year's letter? About one dozen teachers in the room of over 400 teachers raised their hands. In small groups, we discussed why everyone was not saving time this way, and some of the responses were:

- *I cannot find last year's letter in my files without wasting time.*
- *I have a hard copy of the letter; so I will retype.*
- *I know I saved the file, but it is faster to rewrite the letter than look for it.*
- *I never thought about reworking the old letter.*
- *I was at home, and my files were at school.*
- *I did not save the letter last year after I typed it.*
- *I lost everything when my computer crashed.*

This group anxiously listened and created a repurposing plan. With their new organized digital filing cabinets, they are on the road to success.

Based on my work with teachers, I believe the concerns are similar in many school districts. The skill of repurposing is a strategy that must be taught to teachers. Teachers need these timesaving skills.

Activity 6

Repurposing Documents

Follow these simple steps to repurpose a document and use the file again. This is much easier to do after your digital filing cabinet is created and filled with your files and documents.

- Open your new digital filing cabinet and locate your back to school folder.
- Pull out last year's letter by double-clicking on the letter.
- Reread the letter and change the date and a few sentences if needed.
- Another option is to change the clip art to match your theme.
- Save the letter as "Back to School letter to parents 8–03."
- File your new version right back into the same folder next to the old letter.
- Leave the old letter in your file cabinet, it does not take up much space, and you may want to share it with a colleague or student teacher in the future.

Think of all the time you will save next year when you reach into your digital filing cabinet and pull out what you need.

Protect All Your Hard Work

You have created a new system, filed and pitched, and I hope celebrated. Now, this section is designed to protect you from a data disaster. This section will talk about where to save everything. There are options, and this section will help explain the options. The most important message from this section is to back up your data. The how, what, and where will be explained next, but remember to protect your hard work.

WHERE SHOULD I SAVE THINGS? ■

In schools today, there are often more technology options then in the past. Understanding your options and the limitations of each is an important timesaving strategy. Each school system has a different plan for saving. Some schools limit where files can be saved. The tech support team may limit your options. For example, an urban district I often work with does not allow files to be saved to the hard drive; instead they ask staff to use floppies or save to the network.

Wherever you choose to save, do not miss the next section on backing up, a critical step we often do not think about until it is too late.

Which Hard Drive?

- The hard drive on the classroom computer
- The hard drive on another computer in the school
- The hard drive at home

Removable Storage Options

- Floppy disk
- Zip drive
- CD-ROM that you burn
- Removable storage device
- DVD you burn
- USB portable storage device

Other Options

- The school network
- Send the file through e-mail
- Your handheld computer
- On-line storage options

The Hard Drives in Your Life

The hard drive is the piece of hardware within the computer where you save your files and programs. Older computers often have a smaller hard drive than some of the computers available today. There are internal and external hard drives, but most computers today rely on an internal hard drive.

On most computers, the hard drive is labeled with the letter C. My newer home computer has two hard drives, labeled C and D. Between the two hard drives, I have more room for documents, files, and programs than I can ever think of filling.

The hard drive is convenient and available to you whenever you are physically sitting at the computer. The files saved to the hard drive stay on the hard drive. Saving to the hard drive used to be the best place to save files. Today, many of us in a digital world have access to more than one hard drive, and that is when the confusion really sets in.

Sometimes hard drives crash. There are hundreds if not thousands of technical reasons why this happens. To state it simply, if a hard drive crashes, most of the time everything you have on that hard drive is gone. That means that digital filing cabinet you have created and all the files in the filing cabinet are gone. Be prepared by backing up your data. The how-to of backing up data is covered in the next section.

The Hard Drive or Drives in Your Classroom

More and more we are seeing computers in classrooms. One, two, four, seven, or twenty-five hard drives from which to pick. When I started teaching, this is something you could not even imagine. With your machine or machines right there, where should you save?

The most important thing is being consistent. Make a new plan to save in an organized way. A few files on each hard drive soon become a nightmare. If you are lucky enough to have multiple computers in your classroom, you may want to forget the hard drive altogether and save to the school network.

Drawbacks to Relying on the Classroom Hard Drive

Many teachers share classroom space with others, making the classroom computer inaccessible during certain times. Students may also use the computer and accidentally delete your files, read the wrong files, or look at next week's test answers. If you use the classroom computer, make sure your data is protected using a password.

Hard Drives Throughout the Building

How many computers are scattered around your building? Each computer with a hard drive has the potential to save your important document. Without a plan, your data could soon be scattered throughout the school. Soon files of all types are everywhere, labels that do not make sense are common, and no one has any idea of the author of the document.

Drawbacks to Relying on Hard Drives Scattered Throughout the Building

The biggest concern about saving on different computers around the building is losing your files. If you move around from computer to computer, plan to save to the school network. This means your data is not on the local hard drive, but located in your network folder instead. More about using the network is presented in the next section.

The Home Hard Drive

At home, if you have access to a computer, your files are there when you need them. Many busy teachers find the school day is over before they get to use the school computer; so computer work is often done at home. Other teachers may have a Mac at school and a PC at home. This dual platform issue is covered in the chapter on sharing files.

If you often use your home computer as well as a computer at school, you will need to create a digital filing cabinet for home. If other family members also use the same computer, plan for this when you create your home filing system. One of my friends shares her computer with three young sons; a folder for each family member was a big improvement over the original jumbled files. Each person can plan and create subfolders that make sense to them.

Drawbacks to Relying on the Home Hard Drive

The big problem about the home computer hard drive is that it is at home. Imagine you are at the computer late in the evening completing the field trip letter that must go home the next day. The letter is done, spell-checked, and ready to go. You print a hard copy ready for the copy machine. You are off to bed, and the letter is tucked in your school bag. As you are making copies the next morning, your teammate shares a change in the information. You only have a hard copy of the letter, not the digital files, and the letter must go home today. Out of options, you head back to the school computer to retype the letter instead of eating lunch.

There must be a better way to save time. The reality is many teachers must work at home, and the files along with the hard copy must get to school. This leads into the next section about removable storage solutions. Explore these options so that the next time you are working late you will also have what you need the next day at school.

■ REMOVABLE STORAGE

Saving on the hard drive is an option, but it can be difficult to carry a hard drive back and forth. Removable storage is used to transfer data from place to place. Removable storage is often used to back up files. This is covered in the next section. There are many options in removable storage solutions including:

Removable Storage	*Capacity*
A Floppy Disk (sometimes called a Diskette)	1.44MB
A Zip Drive	100 – 250 MB
CD-R or CD-RW	650 – 750 MB
Jazz or Orb Drives	1–2 GB
DVD	4.7 – 9.4 GB
USB Storage Device	8 MB – 2 GB
Compact Flash	4 – 256 MB
MMC Cards	4 – 128 MB
Memory Sticks	4–128 MB

Floppies Everywhere

Many teachers survive by saving everything to floppy disks. Back and forth, to and from school these floppies go. In the Mac world a few years ago, the iMac changed our dependency on floppies. Apple Corporation simply stopped putting a floppy disk drive on the beautiful new machines. This helped many teachers make the transition to saving to the network. Some teachers bought an external floppy and continued to use floppies.

Drawbacks of Using Floppies

Floppies work for short-term transfers of data. However, floppies are easily damaged, and data can be lost forever. Next to me I have a pile of floppies that I failed to label correctly. I could insert each one in my computer, open the files, and delete or save them into my digital filing cabinet. Instead of doing this, my pile gets bigger. Floppies may be needed to transport information back and forth, but make sure to keep a copy of the file on a hard drive or network.

Super Floppy Drives

A Zip drive is a removable storage solution. There are Zip disks that fit into a piece of hardware called a Zip drive. A Zip disk is larger than a traditional floppy and holds more information. There are two kinds of Zip disks which both hold a great deal of data starting at 100 to 250 MB.

To start using a Zip drive, install the software that came with your drive. Attach the drive to the computer using a cable, insert a disk, and you are ready to save to the storage solution. The Zip drive will appear as a choice in "My Computer" on a PC, and on a Mac, an icon will appear on your desktop.

Drawbacks of Super Floppies

You need the hardware and software at home and at school to transfer the data. You could bring the drive back and forth, and it is often in the school bag each day. These disks are more expensive than floppies, and labeling is still critical. Also, if you would like to share with someone else, they also need the hardware to read your disk.

CD-R and CD-RW

CD-ROMs (CD-R) and rewritable CD-ROMs (CD-RW) are becoming an inexpensive easy-to-use storage solution. To "burn" a CD is to take information and write it to a CD-ROM. This CD can then be used in any machine that can read a CD. Cheap and easy to carry around, this is the removable storage solution that works best for me. When I make a presentation, I burn the presentation to a CD-R. With an average cost of approximately 30 cents per CD, I find this is a great removable storage solution.

The rewritable CDs are more expensive at approximately 70 cents per disk, but these disks can be rewritten hundreds of times. This is what I use to back up my files at home. CD-RWs work best on the machine where you "burned" the disk. In traveling between home and school, a better way to do this is to keep the session open on a CD-R and keep adding to it.

Drawbacks

The CD is fragile. CDs can easily be scratched or broken, as I recently experienced.

I was playing high tech volunteer for my son's kindergarten teacher, and I had carefully saved the project to a CD. I put the CD in my bag and went to school. In my bag, the CD cracked in half making it impossible to use. I went back home to burn a new CD, and luckily I had saved a copy in my digital file cabinet on my hard drive.

A New Removable Data Solution

Storage solutions continue to get easier to use and smaller. A new group of products are small enough to hang on your key chain and hold more data than my first computer. These USB solutions are manufactured by a number of companies and are sold under a variety of names. The storage capacity is important in comparing prices. These small storage solutions can hold from 8 MB to 2 GB. USB storage solutons do not need special software installed and can be used on both Apple and PC platforms.

Drawbacks

The size makes the solution great, but what if you lose your keys along with your key chain and your super small digital filing cabinet. Also, not all machines have a USB port, and in some cases, it is not easy to reach the USB port on the back of the computer.

■ NETWORKS

Networks are found in many schools today. The purpose of a network is to share information. Staff and students in the school usually can save files to the network. In most cases, you log on to the network, and this gives you access to a folder with your name on it, as well as a few other shared folders.

A good network can be a huge timesaver. You can save to the network in the same way as outlined earlier for saving to the hard drive. Folders can be created, and you can file things in a folder. One of the best things about working in a networked environment is that most networks are backed up each night onto a tape or CD, giving you that extra peace of mind that your data is safe.

Also, the network enables you to share information with others on the network. You may have a shared folder for teachers where you can store files that are used by several people. If you are part of the fourth grade team, you can have a special folder for all the things you work on together. The network is a powerful way to share resources and collaborate.

Password Do's and Don'ts

Passwords are easy to forget and hard to remember. Passwords must be agreed on, and they are absolutely necessary in a networked environment.

A password is needed to protect your data files. A well-selected password protects your files from hackers who may try to get to your data. Our students are very smart; we need good passwords to protect the tests, assignments, and confidential records we have saved.

Your password is important and needs to be protected. Select something that is easy for you to remember, but difficult for anyone else to predict. A quick guide to selecting passwords can be found on-line at the Jean and Alexander Heard Library at

http://staffweb.library.vanderbilt.edu/libtech/passwd.html

If your school has a network, someone has the job of network administrator. Your network administrator will assign your username. Your username lets the network know who you are, and the password is a security measure to make sure that the user trying to log in is actually you.

Depending how the network is set up, each student in the building may have a folder on the network in which to save files. If this is the case in your building, each student will also have his or her own password. The students can access their network folder anywhere in the building, but not at home. If you have assigned a collaborative assignment for groups to work on, your network administrator may be able to set up a shared folder for the project so that students can share files.

Drawbacks of Saving to the Network

Networks are great, but make sure you know where you save your files. Just like on your hard drive, you need to know where the files are saved. Be consistent.

Also, in some schools, the network server "goes down" on a regular basis. If this is the case at your school, you may also want to save files on your hard drive so that you can access them if the server is "down." Also, you may be in a school without a network. If you are without a "stable network," meaning one that rarely "goes down," your hard drive may be the best place to save things, of course, with a regular plan to back up your data onto floppies or CD-Rs.

A few schools that I work with let you dial into the network from home. Although this is the option in some districts, in many cases it is so slow that it is not worth your time. Most districts do not permit this because of network security. Many districts have a firewall to protect the network and your data from outside uninvited hackers.

Without the ability to dial into the network from home, you need to plan ahead if you will need the documents at home. Before you save the documents, think about when and where you will need to get to that information again.

E-mail Is a Good Solution

E-mail may be a good solution to connect home and school. A document can be sent home as an e-mail attachment, opened and updated, and e-mailed back to school. This is one way to share various types of documents. Many teachers are e-mailing substitute plans from home along with other files needed at schools.

Saving Everywhere

With our scare about the network, floppies, and hard drive crashes, you may be thinking that you should save over and over under different file names. This practice can lead to many problems and wasted time looking for things. Try and be consistent with where and how you save and back up your files on a regular basis. You may choose to add a code into your file name as you save it; for example, the letters "bv" may stand for backup version, "hv" may stand for home version, and so forth.

■ BACKING UP FILES

While researching this section of the book, I read over and over that you should back up on a regular basis and that you should back up in a variety of ways. This means we should not rely on one floppy, CD, or anything else with your important data. Back up often and do this in a variety of ways.

The quickest way to back up data from your school hard drive is to save to the network. In most schools, the files are backed up every night. Check to make sure the back up is being done on a regular basis. Also, if you can, regularly make a back up and store it somewhere other than your classroom. This can be helpful in an emergency, too.

If you have a CD burner at home, this is where I would start. CDs are inexpensive, and the software that came with the computer is usually easy to use. For older machines without CD burners, try borrowing a Zip drive from school to back up the home files. Maybe a new storage solution to back up will help, but do check to see that you have a USB port before heading to the store. The last resort would be use a stack of floppies to back up the data, but in this case, make sure you label everything.

I have not always been on top of my backups, but a nasty recent computer virus has me backing up some important files each week and doing a full backup about once per month. Before you close this guide today, use the following easy steps to start your backup schedule.

The "How-to" of Backing Up Files

These directions will vary depending on what you are saving to.

- Insert the removable storage solution you have selected (CD-R, CD-RW, Zip drive, or network).
- Open your digital filing cabinet and decide what you will back up.
- If you would like to back up your whole digital filing cabinet on a PC, right click on the one main folder (this may be labeled "My Documents") and select "Send To." From this menu, select where you would like this folder to go; for example, CD, floppies, and so forth.
- On a Mac, click on "My Documents" once and drag the folder to the removable storage solution that appears on your desktop. This will copy your files, not delete them from the computer.
- Remove the CD or disk and label and date it carefully.
- Store the CD or disk in a save place. You can relax; your data is safe.

If you have followed along through the chapter, the foundation of timesaving technology has been laid. You have accomplished a great deal as you have developed a stronger digital foundation. Do not be afraid to explore and try new things now that your data is safely backed up.

Some of the news skills you have are:

- Understanding how to save a file
- An organized, efficient digital filing cabinet
- An understanding of your saving choices
- An understanding of the school network
- How to back up your files

Action Plan for Organizing to Save Time

1. How does creating a digital filing cabinet help save time?

2. What documents do you plan on repurposing?

3. Specifically, what is your data backup plan?

4. What have you learned about passwords?

5. What will you add to every file you save from now on?

Copyright © 2004 by Corwin Press, Inc. All rights reserved. Reprinted from *Conquering Infoclutter: Timesaving Technology Solutions for Teachers* by Meghan Ormiston. Thousand Oaks, CA: Corwin Press, www.corwinpress.com. Reproduction authorized only for the local school site that has purchased this book.

Focus Questions for Organizing to Save Time

1. Why should you spend the time to create a digital filing cabinet?

2. Where will you save your new digital filing cabinet and why?

   - Where?

   - Why?

3. What does repurposing your document mean?

4. What is your backup plan to avoid data loss?

5. How will you share information between home and school?

6. What removable storage will you be using to share data?

Copyright © 2004 by Corwin Press, Inc. All rights reserved. Reprinted from *Conquering Infoclutter: Timesaving Technology Solutions for Teachers* by Meghan Ormiston. Thousand Oaks, CA: Corwin Press, www.corwinpress.com. Reproduction authorized only for the local school site that has purchased this book.

5

Managing Technology in the Classroom

Classroom management is a challenge whether you are teaching five-year-olds or fifty-year-olds. Keeping everyone on task and on schedule is difficult. Some of the things an instructor has to keep track of include individual, group, and room schedules. Along with schedules, we have calendars for everything. While juggling all the schedules, plans must be made to meet the individual needs of each learner.

A great organizational system is key. For logistics sake, this chapter focuses on the organizational system and some software products that will help with organization. Strategies for keeping the "administrivia" in order will also be covered. This practical chapter is helpful for everyone from the superintendent to the lunchroom staff.

Self-
Assessment

Self-Assessment for Managing Technology in the Classroom: Where Are You Now?

1. What documents have you repurposed in the last month?

2. List three things you can do to make your documents look professional.

3. How do you use e-mail to save time?

4. What should not be sent through e-mail?

5. How can you organize your e-mail?

6. How could a calendar save time?

7. What tools can you use to streamline planning?

Copyright © 2004 by Corwin Press, Inc. All rights reserved. Reprinted from *Conquering Infoclutter: Timesaving Technology Solutions for Teachers* by Meghan Ormiston. Thousand Oaks, CA: Corwin Press, www.corwinpress.com. Reproduction authorized only for the local school site that has purchased this book.

INFORMATION FLOW ■

There is paper everywhere. Schools are filled with memos, notices, flyers to go home, new schedules, revised schedules, discipline notices, change of address announcements, and of course, the weekly or daily bulletins. No wonder our school bags weigh so much; we have so much "very important paper." I call this infoclutter.

Activity 1

How Does Information Flow in Your School?

This group activity will help your school staff to sort information into two categories: information that needs to be public and information that should be protected. The discussion can be very rich, and it should be open to allow everyone to contribute.

    This activity can be done individually or completed with the entire staff. These are some guiding questions; be open to new ideas. In many schools, the school secretary is the person most people turn to with questions; make sure this key staff member is included in all discussions.

Information Flow at School: An Assessment Tool

What information do teachers need?

Examples: Allergies, medication, health history, parent contact

What information do administrators need that teachers do not?

Examples: Reporting at the state level, performance reviews

What information is confidential?

Examples: Information from the counseling office, personnel files

Copyright © 2004 by Corwin Press, Inc. All rights reserved. Reprinted from *Conquering Infoclutter: Timesaving Technology Solutions for Teachers* by Meghan Ormiston. Thousand Oaks, CA: Corwin Press, www.corwinpress.com. Reproduction authorized only for the local school site that has purchased this book.

What information does the district office need to share?

Examples: Curriculum updates, districtwide committees

What information needs to be shared with administrative staff?

Example: Personnel status, reporting

What information needs to be made available to the public?

Examples: Things to be proud of at school, news releases, good news

What information do students need?

Examples: Homework assignments, links to on-line resources, homework help, and practice schedules

Copyright © 2004 by Corwin Press, Inc. All rights reserved. Reprinted from *Conquering Infoclutter: Timesaving Technology Solutions for Teachers* by Meghan Ormiston. Thousand Oaks, CA: Corwin Press, www.corwinpress.com. Reproduction authorized only for the local school site that has purchased this book.

■ ANALYZE THE INFORMATION FLOW

In most schools, there is a great deal of discussion about access to information for people. Each situation is different, but think about how your network and e-mail could help share information.

Information Flow in the Classroom

There are many things that an individual teacher or school can do to help information flow in a more efficient manner. In the preceding discussion activity, it is best when all sectors of the learning community come together to discuss information flow. Individually or in small groups, the questions let us reflect on the importance of sharing information. This section looks at the flow of information from the standpoint of the classroom teacher and offers ways to streamline and save time.

Classroom teachers have a great deal of data to read, interpret, and process each day in addition to the recordkeeping that accompanies this cumbersome task. Many teachers use technology tools to help them keep everything organized. We will present a variety of ways to help information flow.

Information Flow in the School Office

The life of an administrator is the life of a paper manager. Piles of paper arrive on the desk, and hopefully, piles of paper move out. Conducting the information flow activity as a staff will open a dialogue about new ways to manage information. E-mail is one way to save time, but do not overlook the shared folders.

Committee work is perfect for a shared folder on the network. Everything related to the meetings is stored in this folder. Access to the folder can be limited or open to others. Everything is within reach without heading to the copy machine. Discussing timesaving strategies as a staff is the first step in creating a new system.

■ REUSE DOCUMENTS TO SAVE TIME

Repurposing documents is one of the fundamental skills of timesaving technology. Covered in depth in Chapter 4, teachers could save time repurposing old documents, although finding those documents could be a problem. Here is how to do it.

The Three Musketeers: Cut, Copy, and Paste

Perhaps, the three easiest of the formatting tools are the Cut, Copy, and Paste commands. In order to complete the task of cutting a portion of your document to move elsewhere, simply highlight or select the text. Next, click on the "Cut" button (in Microsoft Office, a pair of scissors located on the standard toolbar.) The highlighted portion disappears. Click on the desired location for the move. Finally, click the "Paste" button (in Microsoft Office, a brown clipboard located on the standard toolbar). Your text reappears in its new location.

The procedure for copying portions of text or graphics is similar. First, highlight or select the text or graphic to copy. Click on the "Copy" button (in Microsoft Office, two white sheets of paper located next to the scissors on the standard toolbar.) Do not be misled when absolutely nothing happens. By clicking on the location for the copied material and then clicking the "Paste" button, your duplicated text or graphic appears.

Repurpose Your Documents

In your files you may have hundreds of things you can repurpose. They may be back-to-school parent notes, weekly or monthly newsletters, units of study, or clip art and photographs. All of these things may be stored on your computer, but without the organization covered in Chapter 4, they may be difficult to spot. Go digital and think about the power of repurposing. Get lots of mileage out of those already-created files.

Sharing is one of the most important lessons we can teach our children, but do not forget about those around you. Think of new ways to pool documents and share resources. Stop doing it the same way we have always done it. Share all those great things hiding in your files.

SHARE THINGS ON THE NETWORK ■

After your staff completes the information flow activity, you should see some trends appear, and you can begin to understand how to effectively distribute information within your building.

Some questions from a recent group include:

- What forms do teachers often request?
- What could you put in a folder on the network and share with staff?
- What data should be kept confidential?
- What does our Acceptable Use Policy (AUP) say?

Focusing on information flow helps schools look at new ways to save time while more effectively sharing information.

Create Professional Documents

With all this sharing and repurposing, make sure that the documents look professional. Be careful if you are not sure about what you are doing in the shared folder. Do not delete files, and remember to say thank you to those that saved you time by sharing resources.

■ SPELL CHECK, GRAMMAR CHECK, SAVE, AND REREAD EVERYTHING

Spell check every document and e-mail. When creating new data documents, it is easy to press the "Print" key before the last edit. Carefully look things over before they go out. Many word processing programs can be set up to spell check automatically. If you use AppleWorks, look for the spell check option on the toolbar or under the Edit menu.

For PC users using the newer versions of Microsoft Word, the little red squiggly line indicates a spelling error. The green squiggly line indicates a grammar error. To fix a spelling error, hold your curser over the red squiggly line and right click your mouse. A menu pops up with spelling options. If the any of the options are correct, select the correct spelling, and the change will be made to your document. This is similar to what will happen by selecting spell check under the Edit menu. This is good to use if you have just a few words to correct at one time.

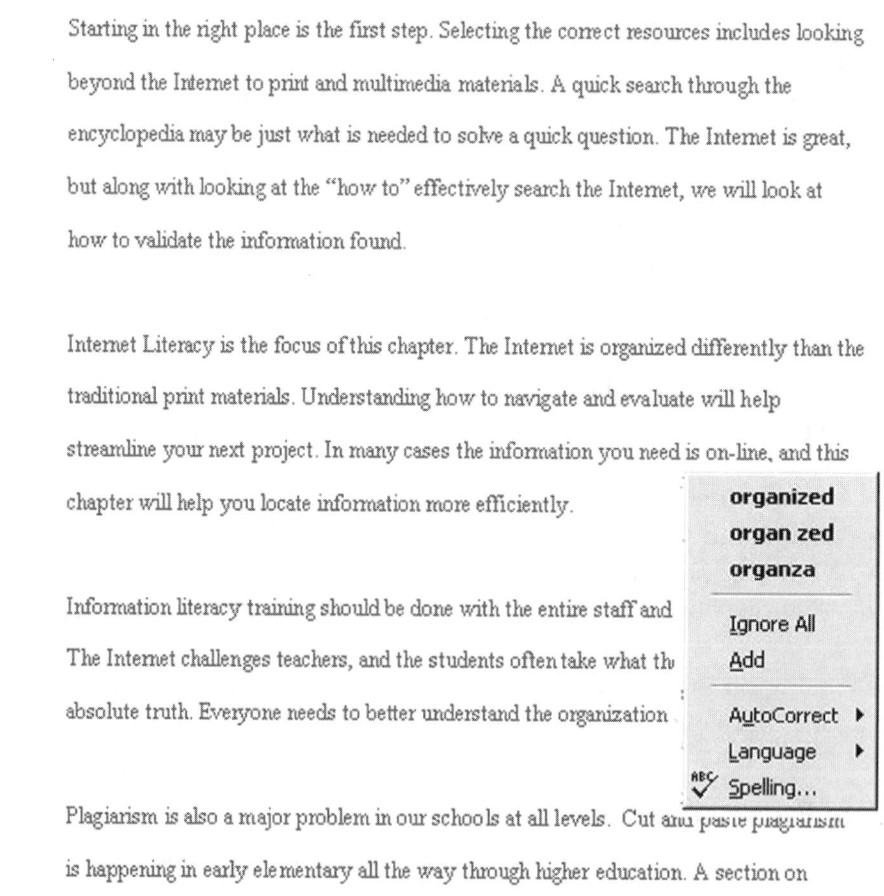

Starting in the right place is the first step. Selecting the correct resources includes looking beyond the Internet to print and multimedia materials. A quick search through the encyclopedia may be just what is needed to solve a quick question. The Internet is great, but along with looking at the "how to" effectively search the Internet, we will look at how to validate the information found.

Internet Literacy is the focus of this chapter. The Internet is organized differently than the traditional print materials. Understanding how to navigate and evaluate will help streamline your next project. In many cases the information you need is on-line, and this chapter will help you locate information more efficiently.

organized
organ zed
organza

Ignore All
Add

AutoCorrect ▶
Language ▶
Spelling...

Information literacy training should be done with the entire staff and The Internet challenges teachers, and the students often take what the absolute truth. Everyone needs to better understand the organization

Plagiarism is also a major problem in our schools at all levels. Cut and paste plagiarism is happening in early elementary all the way through higher education. A section on

Figure 5.1   Right click in Microsoft Word to spell check an individual word

Microsoft Word also has a built-in spelling feature that actually corrects some misspelled words as you type. The program has a built-in feature that actually remembers your spelling mistakes and makes corrections in the future.

While typing documents, a red line may appear below someone's name even though it is spelled correctly. The dictionary does not have that word in it, so the red squiggly line appears. If the person's name is spelled correctly, right click over the red squiggly line and select "Add" from the menu options.

Do not waste time manually spell checking names that you know are spelled correctly. Add the name once, and that name will remain in the dictionary. In Microsoft Office everything is connected, including the dictionary. So when you are working in PowerPoint, the same changes that you have made to the dictionary will also be available there.

Spell Check E-Mail Before Sending It

Most e-mail programs can be set to check spelling before e-mail is sent. If this option is not set, look in the Tools menu for Options and select Spelling. Select "Check e-mail" to check spelling before sending e-mail. In the future, every e-mail will be checked for spelling without selecting the option each time.

Grammar Check and Reread

Checking grammar before saving or sending documents is one way to catch mistakes, but it does not catch everything. Reread or have a friend reread to check for errors. Grammar check misses many things. We need to check it by rereading it in the same manner that we teach students to check everything before turning in an assignment.

Save Everything

The digital filing cabinet you created earlier is ready and waiting for the documents you will create. Save and date everything. To save time, you should do less handwriting of documents and notes. By saving everything you create, you have a running record of all the things you sent home or to another staff member. If something gets lost or if you have questions, you have a backup. Use spell check and grammar check, maybe add some clip art, and file it so you can find the file again. Not only do you look good, but you also have a record.

COMMUNICATION SOFTWARE

In schools today, the two most popular comprehensive electronic mail (e-mail) and scheduling programs available are Microsoft Outlook and Novell GroupWise. Both of these programs are filled with features to help schools communicate effectively. Many of these features only work in schools that are running Microsoft Exchange Server; if your school does not have this program, you may not have access to all the features. Although there are differences in both programs, the main features for both are:

- E-mail
- Contacts
- Tasks
- Appointments
- Scheduling rooms
- Scheduling meetings
- Sharing schedules
- Check school e-mail at home
- Create and share calendars

There are many advanced features in each of the software packages, and many schools are using these programs very creatively. To save time, you could schedule things like visits to the library or computer lab. You could also enter your schedule along with the schedules of other members of a committee and let the program figure out a good meeting time. Assigning tasks to others is another way to delegate and cross some things off your Things to Do List.

These communication programs also allow you to check your school e-mail from home. To do this, you will need a connection to the Internet and a browser. Depending on how your program is set up, you should also be able to schedule rooms and meetings from home.

The power of these software programs allows you to communicate from one fully integrated place. Your school address book can include all the other teachers in the school to save you time. More information can be found on the Internet at the following addresses:

Microsoft Outlook: http://www.microsoft.com/office/outlook/evaluation/guide.htm

Novell GroupWise: http://www.novell.com/products/groupwise/

■ FEATURE COACH COMMUNICATION

Introduction to these integrated packages can be a little overwhelming to new users, but some of the school power users are excited and ready to jump in.

The High Tech Coaches

I was working with a large suburban high school as they rolled out a program giving laptops to each teacher. On the laptops was the newest version of Windows and Microsoft Office. My job was to go through the software and hardware and help teachers make the most of the technology. With over 175 teachers and support staff, we had a big project! The athletic department was very interested in Microsoft Outlook.

The coaching staff at the high school had many great ideas for how to use Microsoft Outlook. With eleven coaches just dealing with football, Microsoft Outlook was the communication tool they were looking for. By quickly creating a distribution list, everyone was receiving the same information. The calendar was another great feature that the athletic director started using right away. The idea of assigning tasks was very popular with the head coach, although we are not sure about the other participants. Communication in this case is the key to a great season!

■ E-MAIL INFOCLUTTER AND SOLUTIONS

Activity 2

E-mail Initial Activity

1. Currently, I am having the following challenges using e-mail:

   a.

   b.

   c.

   d.

2. I would like to learn how to:

   a.

   b.

   c.

   d.

3. How many e-mail messages do you receive each day?

4. Currently, how is your e-mail organized?

5. How do you use your address book?

Copyright © 2004 by Corwin Press, Inc. All rights reserved. Reprinted from *Conquering Infoclutter: Timesaving Technology Solutions for Teachers* by Meghan Ormiston. Thousand Oaks, CA: Corwin Press, www.corwinpress.com. Reproduction authorized only for the local school site that has purchased this book.

E-mail or electronic mail is the lifeline for many educators; for others, it is a management nightmare. Like the introduction of voice mail into school systems, e-mail can get overwhelming. You need practical strategies to take control and make the most of e-mail as a communication tool.

Before discussing saving time with e-mail, the first question is should the information you are sending be sent through e-mail? If you think it is private, start with this section. What does your school district Acceptable Use Policy say about the use of e-mail? A few of the critical questions will be explored in the opening section before we discuss the "how to."

The inbox filled with thousands of old messages is a common problem for e-mail users. We all face the following questions.

Things You Need to Know
Now, Before You Make a Mistake

- What is e-mail etiquette?
- Did you know your e-mail is never private?
- What are viruses and worms?
- How do I stop unwanted e-mail (spam)?
- What about the jokes?
- What are e-mail hoaxes?
- Is your school-sponsored e-mail a matter of public record like other memos in your district?

E-mail Etiquette

There are definite do's and don'ts on-line. These manners are called e-mail etiquette or netiquette, and everyone who e-mails should understand the rules.

There is a whole new etiquette for using e-mail. ARE YOU SHOUTING AT PEOPLE AND NOT REALIZING IT? (using capital letters in e-mail). Are you forwarding things over and over? Are you the novelist everyone dreads getting mail from? This section will help you understand the etiquette e-mail users need.

Netiquette at School

Everyone Has Feelings. Remember there is a human on the receiving end of the e-mail; try not to hurt people's feelings. When we communicate through e-mail, all you see is the computer screen, no body language, gestures, or conversation. Do not send a message when you are angry, and wait a day and reread it carefully before sending it.

Never Type in All Caps. This is considered rude, as if you are yelling at the person to whom you are sending the e-mail message.

Be Polite. Start your e-mail messages with "hello," just like you would on the telephone. Follow up by inquiring as to how the person is before starting the purpose of the e-mail. Complete your e-mail with a closing of thank you, sincerely, or see you soon. Whatever you select, this is a polite way to end your short e-mail.

Look Good On-line. Always spell check a message before sending it. Write in complete sentences and reread your message before you send it. Always capitalize your sentences and use proper punctuation.

Keep It Short and Sweet. Do not be a novelist; people will dread getting mail from you. Get to the point, edit, and send.

Private, No Way

E-mail is not private. A wise person once said that if you would not put it on the bulletin board then do not put it in an e-mail. The message is to be careful with the information that you send through e-mail. E-mail messages are often bounced off different servers, leaving a copy here and there. Without getting technical, the message is to watch what is in your message before hitting "Send."

Confidential information should not be sent through e-mail. Negative comments and observations are better left out of attachments or e-mail. With a click of the button, e-mail can be shared with thousands. Think before you e-mail, and remember e-mail is not for everything.

Make sure you check the Acceptable Use Policy to see if there are limits to what can be sent through e-mail. Good news, celebrations of success, and so forth are great to share with parents; just check that your district does not set limits.

Viruses, Worms, and Other Scary Things

Be careful, and do not open e-mail from someone you do not know. Viruses, worms, Trojan horses, and new things every day can be spread through e-mail. Each one can do something different to your machine causing big and small problems.

An additional prevention could be to install virus scanning software, which is regularly updated to screen incoming and outgoing e-mail for viruses. If you use a laptop computer or a computer at home, be careful and make sure that you have some type of virus protection checking your incoming and outgoing e-mail. If you skipped the section on backing up your data, go back and reread and back up your data today, before a virus affects your computer.

Unfortunately, there are people out there creating these problems. Often they attach to legitimate e-mail or get into someone's address book and send messages from others. Because these viruses and worms are often spread through messages from someone you know, everything should be scanned. In many schools, this is happening long before the e-mail reaches you, but at home you need some type of software scanning incoming and outgoing e-mail.

Spam and Other Annoying E-mail

Spam is unwanted e-mail sent to large numbers of people who would not choose to receive the e-mail message. Most spam is commercial advertising for dubious products or get rich quick schemes. Some people receive hundreds of these messages every day and need to weed through these to get to the important information in their Inbox.

In most e-mail programs, there are ways to deal with spam and hopefully reduce the number of unwanted messages each day. Blocking the sender, creating a message rule, and unsubscribing to the mail are just a few options usually available to you under the Tools menu in your e-mail program.

Unsolicited E-mail and Hoaxes of All Sorts

Along with the spam from people you do not know, you may receive e-mail from people that you do know that carry the latest in e-mail hoaxes. Basically, think of the old chain letters, but now they are on-line. Maybe they have some heartbreaking picture attached. Your friend or colleague passed along the e-mail thinking they are helping someone in need.

I receive these all the time. My friends send them on to me. There are ways to check out these hoaxes to see from where they came.

At Hoaxbusters, you can search for and find many of the same e-mails that you have seen: http://hoaxbusters.ciac.org/

Several other Web sites track this type of thing. Check out the following:

Symantec keeps you on top of some hoaxes: http://www.symantec.com/avcenter/hoax.html

Internet-101.com lists e-mail hoaxes: http://www.internet-101.com/hoax

Datafellows.com is the place to check out virus information: http://www.datafellows.com/news/hoax

UrbanLegends.com is the place to check out the latest urban legends: http://www.urbanlegends.com

These addresses can be shared with students and parents to help verify the many e-mail hoaxes appearing in e-mail inboxes.

Jokes, Stop the Spread of Them

We all have them, the friend or relative who always sends jokes. At home, laugh away. School is a different situation; do not use your school e-mail for jokes. The picture or joke your friend finds hilarious may not be funny if accidentally opened in front of a student or parent volunteer.

Sending jokes through school e-mail actually may be violating the Acceptable Use Policy of the school district. If you do receive a joke, reply to the sender and ask to be taken off the list. If the jokes still keep coming in, delete them instead of sharing the laugh with others in the building. I love a good joke, but skip the school e-mail address just to be safe.

Responding to an E-mail Message From a Group

Be very careful that you know to whom you are sending the mail. In many schools, a message goes out to all staff, and by clicking on "Reply," you will send your message to the entire group. Watch what you say! Many a story can be told of someone accidentally sending e-mail to the wrong recipient. Be careful!

What about groups? You need to communicate with all the second grade teachers or the history department, and groups can make this quick and easy. Setting up and using groups is a huge timesaver, as well as a great way to keep everyone informed.

How would you like your e-mail to stand out from all the others? Examples of creative uses of e-mail will give you some ideas, along with strategies and help for customizing your e-mail messages.

This chapter includes strategies for managing the information flowing through e-mail. The foundation of the timesaving strategies is organization; so we will be looking at ways to bring order to your e-mail.

The Nitty-Gritty of How to Manage E-mail

- How can you tame the Inbox and make it work for you?
- What should be deleted or archived, and how do I do that?
- Instead of everything going to one Inbox, how do I create folders?
- How do you know to whom you sent the e-mail?
- How do I forward an e-mail or copy someone?
- How can I make my e-mail more interesting and fun?

There are specific strategies that will simplify your Inbox, and with some time spent initially, you can even sort e-mail as it comes in.

Taming the Inbox

The Inbox is usually the folder where your e-mail is stored. Just like in your digital filing cabinet, you can create folders within folders in your Inbox. You may have thousands of messages there, or maybe you are just starting out. Organizing this folder is one of the best ways to save time.

Each Inbox can be set up a little differently. For the most part, the messages come into the Inbox, and they appear in bold until you read them. After you read the message, respond, or ignore the message, it remains in the Inbox. Without a system to keep things organized, you quickly could have thousands of messages saved here. If your hard drive has the space, that is fine, but the quantity of messages may be slowing you down.

Figure 5.2   Folders created in the inbox to organize e-mail

Most e-mail inboxes are set up in a similar way. First, it shows the person's name that sent you the e-mail, and next, it shows the subject of the e-mail and the date and time the message was received. To read one of the messages, double click to open the message. After reading the message, the options along the top are to "Forward" the message, "Delete" the message, "Reply" to the message, and "Reply All," if the message was sent from a group.

Creating Folders in Your Inbox

Plan before you start creating folders. Think back to the ideas covered in the section on the Digital Filing Cabinet. You can use the same plan here. Start with no more than four or five large categories. Folders within folders work in the same way as your data folders. Record your plan to tame your Inbox.

Activity 3

My Plan to Tame the Inbox

1. My four or five large categories will be:

   a.

   b.

   c.

   d.

   e.

2. What subfolders may I need?

3. My plan for cleaning up my Inbox is:

4. What is in your Inbox that you can delete?

5. What is in your Inbox that should be saved?

Copyright © 2004 by Corwin Press, Inc. All rights reserved. Reprinted from *Conquering Infoclutter: Timesaving Technology Solutions for Teachers* by Meghan Ormiston. Thousand Oaks, CA: Corwin Press, www.corwinpress.com. Reproduction authorized only for the local school site that has purchased this book.

CREATE YOUR E-MAIL ■ DIGITAL FILING CABINET

Each e-mail program has different features. Most of the programs allow you to make folders within the Inbox. On a PC computer, right click on the Inbox label and a dialogue box appears with a new folder option. Select this option and name your folder.

Start with your four or five large topics. After these folders are made, use the same procedure to add any subfolders you would like.

Different Views and Layouts

There are different views of your Inbox depending on your e-mail program. Most often the option is found under the View menu. Experiment to see which view works best for you. If you are creating folders and folders within folders, you may want a view of the folders. Turn off the Preview Pane to protect yourself from e-mail viruses; many of the new viruses can run just by appearing in the Preview Pane. To do this, go to the View menu and select "Layout" and then select "Preview Pane."

Deleting a Message in the Inbox

Get rid of the junk e-mail and the other e-mail you do not need to keep by deleting the message. You delete only when you are done with the message and you do not need to save it "for the record." The quick way to delete the message on a PC computer is to put the curser over the message to delete and right click the mouse button. When you do this, a menu pops up, and you can select "Delete." The message goes to the "Deleted Items" folder.

Delete things you do not want in your Inbox such as jokes someone sent you. File the messages in the new e-mail Digital Filing Cabinet you have created. Keep any files to which you may need to refer. Your Inbox is a great recordkeeper for you and is very helpful if someone needs a copy of a message. It is not bad to keep things in your Inbox, but due to space issues, your district may ask you to limit the number of messages in your Inbox. Ask your network administrator about the best way to manage your messages; each system is set up differently. Ask about where your messages are stored on the server or your local hard drive.

TACKLE THE MESS YOU HAVE ■

The manual way to clean up is to drag and drop to add messages to your new folders. Start with the most recent e-mails and delete the messages no longer needed. For important e-mail, drag the message to the new folder you have created. This is one way to do this, but let us explore a timesaving way to do this.

Automated Cleanup

Make your e-mail program do the cleanup for you. Most e-mail programs have filters or rules that you can create to organize e-mail. You can go through and create rules directing the incoming e-mail into one of the folders you have created. Once the rule is created, you can run the rules, and the software will file the old messages into the folders you designate. In the future, new e-mail that matches the rule will not come into your general e-mail Inbox, but instead will go into the designated folder. You will know that you have mail because that folder will be bold until it is read.

This timesaving strategy also helps by managing incoming mail that I do not want to read such as the spam covered earlier. Once e-mail starts coming in that I do not want to receive again, I create a rule to delete messages from this source. This helps you keep a record of important e-mails in one folder and helps tame the Inbox.

■ ADDRESS BOOK

Your Address Book is where all your contact information can be stored. Depending on the e-mail program you use, the options will vary. Most programs allow you to include contact information along with e-mail addresses.

Your Address Book is a huge timesaver if it is organized and working for you. In the address line, start typing a name, and a box filled with names that match what you are typing appears. If you keep typing, you can select the full name from the list. Another way to select someone is to open the Address Book and select the name from the list. You can select one or more names from your Address Book by selecting additional names.

Most address books can also be organized and printed in a variety of ways. Labels for holiday cards, announcements, and invitations can be printed right from your Address Book. One newer feature of my e-mail program is a link to an on-line map of the address I have added, a huge timesaver for me. My Address Book saves me hundreds of hours each year.

Some of the Address Book options may include:

- Home and business addresses
- Web site addresses
- Telephone, fax, cell phone numbers
- Conferencing information
- Notes
- Personal information
- Map of location

Creating Groups

The quick way to send a message to more than one person at a time is to establish a group or distribution list. In a school setting, you may want to make a group for each grade level or department. A classroom teacher

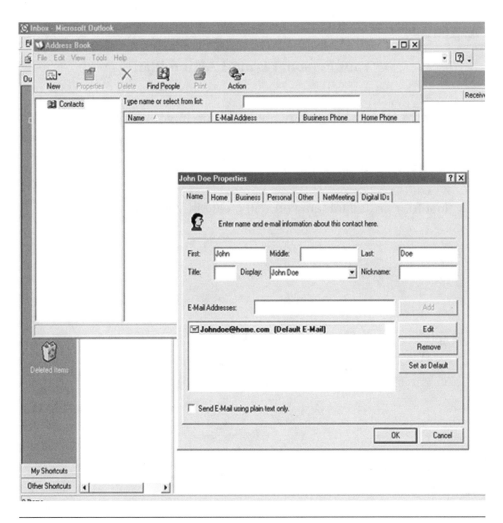

Figure 5.3 Add a contact to the address book

may make a group of parent e-mail addresses. Create a group by opening your Address Book and looking for a "create group" feature. Add or select names to add to the group.

If you plan on creating and using groups, make sure group members understand that everyone can read any messages sent to the group. If you receive a message from a group, by hitting "Reply" you are responding to the group, not an individual. Be careful here! Make sure your response is appropriate for the group; if not, select the individual you would like to reply to and send a new e-mail message.

More Timesaving Tips

Most e-mail programs come with a Help feature. Many programs also come with a tutorial you can work through. I also pick up a book now and then to look for new ways to streamline my e-mail Inbox; a few of these resources are listed in the Bibliography. The time spent organizing your e-mail Digital Filing Cabinet will save you time each and every day.

Try it Out Activity!

Activity 4

Your Personal E-mail Action Plan

1. Approximately how many messages are in your Inbox currently?

2. List four or five folders you will create in your e-mail Inbox.

   a.

   b.

   c.

   d.

   e.

3. What rules do you plan on creating?

4. What groups could you create to save time?

5. What should you remember when you reply to a group e-mail message?

6. Where can you get more help?

Copyright © 2004 by Corwin Press, Inc. All rights reserved. Reprinted from *Conquering Infoclutter: Timesaving Technology Solutions for Teachers* by Meghan Ormiston. Thousand Oaks, CA: Corwin Press, www.corwinpress.com. Reproduction authorized only for the local school site that has purchased this book.

PLANNING TO INCLUDE TECHNOLOGY ■

Calendars

On-line, on the network, or on paper, calendars are a good way to organize and share information. There are many ways technology can help you create and share your calendars. With all the information that needs to be organized, you need a variety of tools.

On the Internet, there are a number of Web sites where you can create your own calendars. Depending on the information you would like to put on the calendar, the Internet is a great place to publish. By publishing on the Internet instead of just printing on paper, parents can access information anywhere that they can access the Internet. Remember your Acceptable Use Policy about what can and cannot be published on-line.

There are also a few other on-line calendars that are not specifically designed for education. These calendars are very powerful, and you can choose who has access. Examples of general calendars include:

Yahoo calendar site: http://www.calendar.yahoo.com

MSN calendar site: http://www.calendar.msn.com

One thing to watch is advertising on the Web site. If students will be checking the calendar, make sure the advertising is appropriate.

Many schools and districts post a calendar on their Web site. The calendars come in many formats from a simple list to full color calendars. Many of the Web page authoring software programs give you the tools to create your own calendars. A few of the calendars may include:

- School calendars
- Lunch menus
- Sports schedules
- After school activities
- Building-based events
- School Board meetings
- Parent group information

SIMPLE CALENDARS AND ■
SCHEDULES FOR PREREADERS

Software to Make Calendars

You can also make the most of the software on your computer to generate your own calendars. In Microsoft Office and AppleWorks or ClarisWorks there are templates available to generate your own calendars. These templates can be modified to meet your specific needs. Some of our favorite calendar programs include:

Microsoft Publisher	The wizards make it very easy to walk through each step.
Microsoft Outlook	Your calendar is part of a comprehensive management program.
Calendar Creator by	This is easy to use and has a wide variety of features. Broderbund
Novell GroupWise	Your calendar is part of a comprehensive management program.

Calendar for the '02-'03 School Year.

August	26-27	Teacher Institute Days
	28	First Day of Classes for Students
September	2	Labor Day Holiday
	27	Mid-Quarter
October	11	Teacher Institute Day
	14	Columbus Day Holiday
	15	Teacher Institute Day
November	1	End of 1st Quarter (44 days)
	8	Report Cards
	14	Parent-Teacher Conferences, 5:30-8:30 p.m.
	15	Parent-Teacher Conferences, 8:30-11:30 a.m.
	27-29	Thanksgiving Break
December	7	Mid-Quarter
	20	Winter Break begins at 3:05 p.m.
	23-31	Winter Break
January	1-3	Winter Break
	6	Classes resume
	20	Martin Luther King, Jr.'s Birthday Holiday
	22	End of Semester (2nd Quarter) (43 days)
	31	Report Cards
February	13	Parent-Teacher Conferences, 5:30 p.m. - 8:30 p.m.
	14	Parent-Teacher Conferences, 8:30 a.m. - 11:30 a.m.
	17	Presidents' Day Holiday
	28	Mid-Quarter

Figure 5.4   A school year calendar

■ LESSON PLAN BOOKS

Many teachers use computers to organize and plan lessons. Using technology enables you to hyperlink to resources on-line and on file within your word processing table, thus streamlining the planning process. At the elementary and middle schools, filling out lesson plan books each week is an expectation by most administrators.

The daily schedule including specials, lunch, recess, and dismissal times are added each week by the teacher, the same thing over and over. To

Pete's Schedule

Monday	Art	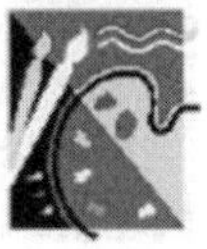
Tuesday	Skills for growing	
Wednesday	Gym	
Thursday	Gym & Show and Tell	
Friday	Library & Music	

Figure 5.5　A simple calendar for a non-reader

streamline the process, a template can be created and additional specific information can be added each week (see Figure 5.6). By completing the template once, this master can be used on the computer or as a guide when handwriting lessons.

Many more templates for lesson plans can be found on-line at http://www.techteachers.com/templates.htm

The following is an elementary lesson plan example.

A MIDDLE SCHOOL EXAMPLE ■ OF AN ASSIGNMENT PAGE

Each teacher has access to a homework and assignment template that they can quickly fill in, and with a click of a button, the homework is posted to a central site on the school Web site. The technology director at this school meets with the teachers and creates a password-protected form for the teachers. This form can be accessed from home or school, and teachers can update it as often as necessary (see Figure 5.7 for example).

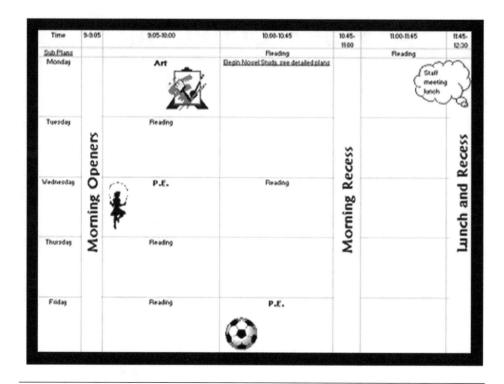

Figure 5.6   A lesson plan template

■ LONG-RANGE PLANNING

Everything starts with planning. Technology is often pushed aside to allow time to cover more content from the textbook. Creating a plan based on standards is the key. The textbook is one tool to deliver curriculum. Plan to include technology as a critical element to your unit of study.

Technology will save teachers time in planning. The paper plan books have limits; so let us explore ways to use technology to make your plans look great and save time.

All planning should start by asking essential questions. Once the essential questions have been asked, the next step is to identify standards to be included in planning. The textbook does not drive the curriculum. The standards drive the curriculum. This is critical to planning and assessing and aligning curriculum.

I have been working with an elementary district for about five years, consulting, planning, and working with small groups of teachers throughout the year. This project has been an exciting one! Each teacher in the project has four to five networked computers in their classrooms along with a printer and scanner. My work with this group has been redefining curriculum and helping integrate technology. Throughout the school year, we meet in grade-level teams and share and create units to take back and use throughout the year.

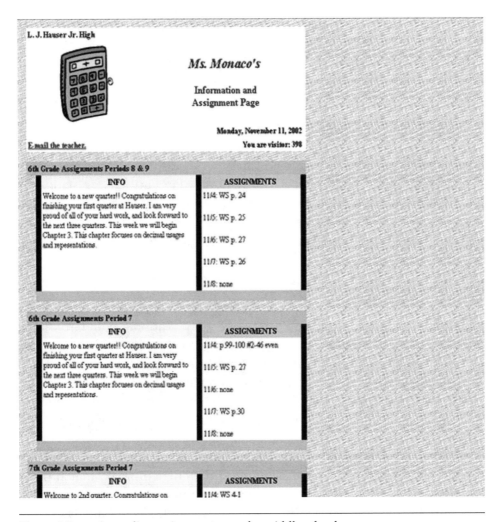

Figure 5.7   An on-line assignment page for middle school

Each spring we get together and do long-range planning for the following school year. During a recent meeting, using "The Technology Integration Year at a Glance Planning Grid," most grade levels were busy filling in the grid and discussing the sequencing of the curriculum. One group was working quietly in the corner, but was at a loss for what to put in the grid. This group was getting a new textbook and did not yet know the curriculum.

After a great discussion of standards driving the curriculum, the textbook as a tool to support standards, and technology to help, we started mapping out the year. We used the standards and their many years of experience to plan out the year. During our next meeting, we had the new textbook and materials, and we were able to fill in the empty holes in the grid. Based on our plan, the book was not taught exactly in the sequence the publisher recommended, but the plan was well developed and aligned to the state expectations.

This is a talented team of teachers reacting in the way most teachers do when a textbook series changes. The standards did not change the stories, projects, or activities they may have. Standards need to drive the planning and the curriculum delivery in the classroom. If the textbooks are not designed to meet the specific standards of your curriculum, we need to plan for this.

■ IT ALL STARTS WITH THE STANDARDS

Each year more students are subject to high stakes tests. These tests have been created based on local, state, or national standards. These standards should drive curriculum in the district. There are many on-line resources to help you identify standards, along with lesson plans and resources. These Web sites can be big timesavers for teachers who are realigning curriculum.

Which Standards?

"Whose standards" is the critical question. National standards have been created in a number of content areas including mathematics, social science, and technology. Many states have used these national standards as they create the state standards. State standards are then used to align curriculum in many districts. Because standards vary from state to state, many textbook companies align to national standards with supplemental guides for each state.

Aligning to the standards should be done throughout the year, not just the few weeks before the test. Realigning the curriculum to match these standards takes time. Many districts have committees to create guides for other teachers in the district. In smaller districts, this is not always possible and leaves the challenge to the classroom teacher.

Often you will find the standards or local curriculum in a very important binder that you are handed at the beginning of the year and check back in at the end of the year. The standards and critical information in the binders need to translate into effective instruction throughout the year.

■ PLANNING TOOLS

I have designed a number of planning tools to help you pull all of this together to plan based on standards and to infuse technology when it supports teaching and learning.

Plan to save time by collaborating with other teachers at the same grade level. Revisit other chapters for specific ways to share resources to save time using your school network and shared files.

Customize the plans to meet specific needs. The planning grids work best when they are customized. Each school has specific requirements that need to be included in planning. These grids were created in a spreadsheet program, but a table in a word processing program would also work. I

	August	September	October	November	December	January	February	March	April
Monthly Activities	Introduce management, procedures, and on-line resources	Morning Openers Weather	Pumpkin Poetry and author study	Virtual Field Trip to the Mayflower (Scholastic Network)	e-mail Santa, spreadsheets of gift lists, millennium predictions	Presidents use the Kids National Geographic site, millennium	Send electronic valentines, Black History Month	Author Studies on-line	Take a trip around the world virtually
Student skills	Logging on to the server, saving	Spreadsheet use integrated into our Data collection unit in math	Word processing	Presentations	Desktop Publishing	Internet Research, searching	Documenting Internet Resources	Selecting the appropriate resource	Multimedia
Professional Development Goals	start a technology portfolio	Internet resources	Multimedia presentations	Digital Imaging	Improve Internet searching	Create an e-mail newsletter to parents	Create a web page	Organize bookmarks	Share ideas colleagues
Curriculum									
Language Arts		Literature Circles	Historical fiction	Author Study	Fiction	Author Study	Fairytales	research	Author Study
Math	Real Life Problem Solving	Data Collection	Place value	Time and money	Addition	Subtraction	measurement and probability	Multiplication	Geometry
Science	The scientific process		Magnetism		Plants		Animals		Earth
Social Studies	My Family			My Neighborhood		The community		The world around us	
Other									
Projects	My Family			Person of the Century		My Community		The World Around Us	
Activities within the project		timelines, time capsule, primary source documents, family trees		Select a person of the century and make a multimedia		Map making, researching, integrate study of architecture		research on-line and off,	
Assessment									
Standards									

Figure 5.8   An example of a planning grid, more found at www.infoclutter.com

often print them out on legal size paper. In small groups, we handwrite things in the boxes, and many teachers then fill in the boxes on the spreadsheet. I also add hyperlinks to files, units, games, or Web sites that are part of my plan. For me, the hyperlinks are a great way to save time.

CHALLENGE STUDENTS OF ALL ABILITIES ■

Of all the management jobs in the classroom, the most challenging is meeting the diverse needs of all learners. In your classroom, you may have students who are years ahead or behind the rest of the class in some areas. How do you meet the needs of all students?

In the past, teachers poured over catalog titles ordering software to help boost basic skills in all content areas. If there was money to purchase the software, it was ordered and shipped to the technology coordinator. The software often sat unused for many months of the year, or it may still be on that shelf.

Software site licenses can be very expensive, and some software titles are not compatible with the changing school hardware. Installing all the software and having it available for students is another challenge. Storage closets and shelves are filled with software titles no one is using. Many free on-line resources are found on the companion website.

■ MAKE A PLAN TODAY TO SAVE TIME

Included in this chapter are many ways to save time. The Information Flow worksheet helps everyone in the school system look at new ways to save time. Technology can also help everyone be more professional. Spell check, grammar check, repurposing, and saving files are some strategies explored in depth.

**Action Plan for Managing
Technology in the Classroom**

1. How can repurposing documents save you time?

2. What can you do to make your documents look professional?

3. How can e-mail save you time?

4. Specifically, regarding e-mail what have you learned?

   a.

   b.

   c.

5. What types of calendars could you create to save time?

6. What tools will you use to save time in planning?

Copyright © 2004 by Corwin Press, Inc. All rights reserved. Reprinted from *Conquering Infoclutter: Timesaving Technology Solutions for Teachers* by Meghan Ormiston. Thousand Oaks, CA: Corwin Press, www.corwinpress.com. Reproduction authorized only for the local school site that has purchased this book.

**Focus Questions for Managing
Technology in the Classroom**

1. Why is it important to analyze how information flows at school?

2. How can documents look more professional?

3. How can the effective use of communication software save time?

4. What are three important e-mail etiquette points to remember when e-mailing?

5. How can you help prevent the spread of viruses?

6. Where can you go to find out if the e-mail sent to you is a hoax?

7. What planning tools would be helpful to teachers?

Copyright © 2004 by Corwin Press, Inc. All rights reserved. Reprinted from *Conquering Infoclutter: Timesaving Technology Solutions for Teachers* by Meghan Ormiston. Thousand Oaks, CA: Corwin Press, www.corwinpress.com. Reproduction authorized only for the local school site that has purchased this book.

6

Publishing Globally

You can do it, that is, publish globally. This chapter moves you on-line. In walking through the process step-by-step, you will have concrete, specific strategies to use for posting resources to the World Wide Web. Starting with organizing bookmarks, the practical solutions are here for you to share with your students, as well as with other teachers across the globe.

Self-
Assessment

Self-Assessment for Publishing Globally: Where Are You Now?

1. How are you currently organizing Web sites you find valuable?

2. Specifically, what would help you save time?

3. What does your Acceptable Use Policy say about posting to the Internet?

4. If your school has a Web site, how can you post to it?

5. What would you like to post on the Internet?

6. What are your concerns about posting to the Internet?

Copyright © 2004 by Corwin Press, Inc. All rights reserved. Reprinted from *Conquering Infoclutter: Timesaving Technology Solutions for Teachers* by Meghan Ormiston. Thousand Oaks, CA: Corwin Press, www.corwinpress.com. Reproduction authorized only for the local school site that has purchased this book.

ORGANIZING WEB SITES ■

Bookmarks or Favorites

Bookmarks, favorites, files of Web sites, index cards, or sticky notes with Web site addresses are everywhere. This section looks at how to organize all these great resources so you can find them again.

Organizing bookmarks or favorites is where we start. Creating your own Web site comes next. This section is filled with examples from the Internet to inspire you and give you practical starting points.

The goal of saving time will not be a reality if you cannot get back to the Web sites you need. Bookmarks or favorites help us do just that. It is rarely a good idea to have an entire class "surfing" the Internet. To make the most of each teachable moment, we need to direct students to resources and move on with the curriculum.

The use of bookmarks on every computer also has implications that are discussed in this section. Making the most of class time is important, and we do not want to waste time with students typing in addresses. Keep it digital and keep it simple.

Bookmarks or favorites are a great feature built into your Web browser. For Netscape users, the term is Bookmarks, and for Internet Explorer users, the term is Favorites. With all the different labels, they all do approximately the same thing. These features keep the Web sites you identify in a list so that you can select them and go directly to the Web sites.

The next time you want to go back to a particular Web site, go back to your Favorites list and locate the Web site to visit, select it, and you are connected to that Web site. Is it a great way to record your Web sites?

Limitations of Bookmarks or Favorites

As helpful as this feature is there are a few limitations. In most schools when you log on to a computer on the network that is not your usual computer, your bookmarks do not "come with you." When you want to go down the hall and share your newly found Web site, your bookmark stays back on the computer in your room. Some school networks have been set up so that your bookmarks go with you to whatever computer you may be using on the school network.

Your bookmarks stay only on your computer. Now, back at your main computer you may have hundreds and hundreds of bookmarks on that computer in a huge list. You look over the list to find the Web site that you need for your lesson, and it is lost among the other hundred or so poorly named bookmarks. You are not saving time.

For all those bookmarks you have, time is needed to organize them. Other strategies are explored in the next section. For now, you need to weed the bookmarks and organize the good ones. In the next section, we give you specific instructions for your browser.

Netscape Navigator or Internet Explorer

Your browser is the software used to look at the World Wide Web. The two main browsers used in schools are Internet Explorer and Netscape Navigator.

In this section, the browser version you are using should not make a difference. When you launch the Internet browser, look for either the Internet Explorer icon or the Netscape Navigator icon to identify your browser. Use the browser with which you feel comfortable. There are a few differences, but both programs get you to the Internet.

Organizing Favorites in Internet Explorer

Open up the browser and look for a Web site. If you would like to add this particular Web site to your favorites, start by clicking on the Favorites folder on the toolbar. This opens the side frame on the left. Click on "Add to Favorites," and a box pops up with some features that you can use to organize your favorites.

In the white box, you will see the name of the Web site as it will appear in your favorites list. You can change this Web site name to something that makes sense to you. Another feature is the "Make available offline" feature. This feature allows you to view the Web site when you are not connected to the Internet. This is a good feature for those schools with less then stable Internet access. This feature can use a lot of hard drive space based on the file size. Be careful here. Once you click on the OK button, the favorite has been stored in your list.

Organizing Bookmarks in Netscape Navigator

After discovering a Web site that you would like to save, go the Bookmarks menu and select "Add bookmark." The bookmark is added to your list. To organize the list from the Bookmarks menu, select the "Go to bookmarks" option. Here you can create folders, delete, rename, and organize your bookmarks.

■ ORGANIZING FAVORITES IN INTERNET EXPLORER

Just like your organizational plan for your data files and e-mail inbox, start with four or five main topics. Now that you know how to create bookmarks, you may soon have a huge disorganized list. This section helps you organize those favorites into folders.

In the left frame in the Favorites window, there is an "Organize Favorites" option. Click on "Organize Favorites," and a dialog box appears. The options to "Create Folder" or "Delete" will help you organize your Favorites list. Click on "Create Folder." Name your new folder.

As a classroom teacher, you may have a folder for each subject that you teach. For example, once you have a mathematics folder, you can also create subfolders for major topics such as geometry, whole numbers, and so forth. While in this "Organize Favorites" dialogue box, you can drag Web sites into your folder.

After you complete the task of going through your favorites, in the future you will want to be more organized when you save a Web site. At the time that you are about to create a favorite, file it in the right folder instead of adding it to the large list. This will keep your favorites organized and will save you time.

The Computer Lab and Bookmark, or Favorite, Nightmare

Many teachers rely heavily on bookmarks or favorites to direct students to specific Web sites in the classroom or computer lab. In a computer lab setting, the Web site needs to be bookmarked at each computer. When students enter the computer lab, they select the bookmark and go to the Web site.

This is a way to save time and help students find the Web sites, but that is a lot of extra work for the instructor. Bookmarks or favorites are great, and now you may be ready for the next step of sharing those Web sites with others.

SHARE THOSE WEB SITES WITH OTHERS ■

As you explore the Internet, you may find a Web site for a colleague. Try to avoid the impulse to hit "Print" and insert it in the colleague's mailbox. Instead, send the page or link to your colleague. In both Internet Explorer and Netscape Navigator, under the File menu there is a "Send" command. Select send "Page by e-mail," and an e-mail box pops up ready for you to send the page to your colleague.

Your colleague will appreciate this because all he or she has to do is click on the link to the Web page with no typing or mistyping. By using your address book, you can send the Web page to more than one person at a time.

Hyperlinks Everywhere

More advanced than the use of bookmarks is to compose a word processing document and copy and paste Internet addresses (URLs) into the document. In some word processors, this creates an automatic hyperlink, and usually turns the font color of the address blue. This means that when you click on the address that your Internet browser window opens and takes you to the Web site. Another quick solution is to save the document into the shared folder so that others can make use of the document.

To Copy Web Addresses to a Word Processing Document:

- Locate a Web address to which you would like to direct students.
- In the address bar, copy the address.
- Open the word processor.
- Select "Paste" from the Edit menu.
- Press the space bar or "enter."
- Type the address of the Web site name as it appears on the Web page and hit "enter."
- To remember what is located on the Web site, type a description of what is on the Web site.
- Continue to cut and paste Web addresses.
- Save the document and file in your digital filing cabinet.

If you would like students to access these Web sites, they can be saved in a shared folder on the school network. To make it possible to have multiple students open the document at one time, select "Read Only" when saving. If "Read Only" is not selected, only one student will be able to access the document at a time.

Preselecting Resources for Students

Selecting resources for students is critical. Having students searching for Web sites can be a waste of time. Even in schools that use filtering software, students may also discover something inappropriate on-line. Plan where students go by saving Web sites.

Creating a document and saving it on the network is one way to streamline the use of the Internet. The only problem with this method is that students can only use this document at school where they can access the network.

■ READY TO GRADUATE TO THE BIG TIME: YOUR OWN WEB SITE

You have organized bookmarks, you have created word processing documents filled with Internet sites on the school server, and you have shared Internet resources with colleagues via e-mail. You are ready to graduate to the big time. The big time is your own Web page or Web site.

Creating a Web site sounds like a huge task, but the truth is that if you can type it, scan it, or snap a digital picture of it, you have what you need to create a Web site. Just think of a Web site as pages that are organized and connected by links. Start small and then you can expand your site. Simplify your life and save time.

Your digital filing cabinet is working for you now. Organizing all the Web addresses you use is the same concept. When I started out, I had no idea as to how to create a Web page. Today, I am the Web master of several hundred pages in one very large Web site. Remember that if it is digital, it can be a Web page.

Roadblocks

The biggest roadblock for teachers is time. Luckily in the past few years things have been simplified. Do not worry about fancy graphics or fonts. All of that can be explored in the future. For now, the goal is to save time by organizing on-line resources.

Previously, you needed to know how to "code" to create a Web page. This means you knew HTML and all the confusing symbols that went with it. HTML is the language of the Internet. Everything must be saved in HTML to be posted on the Internet. Now there is easy to use editing software available so that you can add your information simply by typing it, and the software automatically adds the coding. There are also on-line options and software options that we will explore.

Before You Continue, Know Your Acceptable Use Policy

Most districts have an Acceptable Use Policy concerning technology and use of the Internet. In some districts, this policy limits what can be posted on-line. Every district is different; make sure you know what can and cannot be posted on-line.

Are you ready to create your own Web page? We have a few questions to ask before we proceed.

Activity 1

Publishing Planning Guide

1. Does your school have a Web site? If so, answer the following questions:

   a. Are you permitted to publish your own home page?

   b. What is the procedure for this?

   c. Where can you get help?

2. If you do not have the ability to publish Web sites at school:

   a. Do you have Internet access at both home and school?

   b. Who will be accessing your Web site?

   c. For what will you use this Web site?

3. Are you ready to create and publish your own Web site?

   a. Do you want to use a template?

   b. What software do you have?

Activity 2

Content Planning Guide

1. What is the purpose of your Web site?

2. How will you use this Web site with:

   a. Students?

   b. Parents?

   c. Colleagues?

3. How will you organize the Web site?

4. What Web pages do you want included?

5. How often do you plan on refreshing the content on your Web page?

Copyright © 2004 by Corwin Press, Inc. All rights reserved. Reprinted from *Conquering Infoclutter: Timesaving Technology Solutions for Teachers* by Meghan Ormiston. Thousand Oaks, CA: Corwin Press, www.corwinpress.com. Reproduction authorized only for the local school site that has purchased this book.

PUBLISHING OPTIONS FOR YOUR WEB PAGE ■

If the Web page sounds like a good idea, before beginning you need to have a plan to publish the Web page or pages to the Internet. These pages are different than your data files that are saved to the network. To be viewed by the world your Web pages need to be on a "Web server," a computer that is always connected to the Internet. For your new Web page, you have four options:

Option 1. Your school has a Web site, and the school Web master posts your changes.

Option 2. Your school does not have its own Web site, and you want to post your Web pages for free.

Option 3. You are willing to pay a small fee for posting your Web site.

Option 4. You are willing pay a fee for your Web site and have complete control.

Option 1: The School Has a Web Site and the School Web Master Posts Your Changes

Many schools have some type of Web site, but in many cases, this is not an active Web site. Many schools have posted a few Web pages filled with basic information. School Web sites need to be updated to bring people back. A Web page that is not updated is like the bulletin board that stays the same all year. Some schools have very active Web pages, logging in thousands of Web page views each day.

If your school has a Web site with space available to you, this is the best way to proceed. Many districts have a staff member that serves as the Web master. There may be a specific procedure that needs to be followed before Web pages are posted, including a review for spelling, grammar, and content.

If teachers will be creating Web pages, software is needed. A good Web site for beginners that is filled with templates and backgrounds is Web Workshop by Sunburst located at

http://www.sunburst.com/schoolhouse/webworkshop/

This is a good beginning for teachers as well as students publishing on-line.

For those teachers using Apple computers, the favorite software for many is Adobe Go Live. This software is filled with advanced features as well as templates for the beginner to use to get started. The Web address is

http://www.adobe.com/products/golive/main.html

Option 2: The School Does Not Have Its Own Web Site, and You Want to Post Your Web Pages for Free

There are many Web sites that will post your Web pages for free. However, the number of these Web sites has dropped dramatically. The Web sites make money by selling advertising on your Web pages and throughout the Web site. As advertising revenues declined, many of the free Web hosting companies are no longer in business or now charge for the service of posting your Web pages.

A Word About Advertising

With all of the options listed, there will be advertising on your Web pages. This may bother some people, but remember this Web site is free. For most of the Web sites that are available specifically for teachers, screen the advertising carefully. If students will be accessing your Web site, keep a close watch on the advertising.

Web Sites to Investigate for Free Web Hosting

The Web sites that are free have templates which you fill out, and then, with a click of a button, your information is posted to the Internet. You have many options to get started. After registering and setting up your Web site, a click of the button will have you published in a matter of minutes. Each of the following Web sites reviewed have free as well as low-cost packages.

The world's largest free space provider, with over 5 million "Homesteaders," is located at http://geocities.yahoo.com/

The second largest free Web hosting site is located at http://www.tripod.lycos.com/guides/move.html

Angelfire is now part of Lycos and is located at http://www.angelfire.lycos.com

Top cities is open for everyone and is located at http://www.topcities.com

Option 3: You Are Willing to Pay a Small Fee for Posting Your Web Site

These Web sites may no longer be free, but without a school Web server, this may be an option. There are many Web sites available for a low fee; one Web site that I have used extensively is Family Education Network's My School Online located at http://www.myschoolonline.com/golocal

Currently there is a thirty-day free trail and an annual fee of approximately $30.00.

Option 4: You Are Willing to Pay a Fee
for Your Web Site and Have Complete Control

Your Own Web Site Domain

A Web site domain is your Web address. A school Web site may have a long Web address assigned by a state organization such as http://www. district96.w-cook.k12.il.us or http://www.oakland.k12.mi.us. Like a vanity license plate, a Web site domain is a great way to personalize a Web site. Recently, I found several teachers with new Web site domain names and great Web sites. This is a great way to showcase the many things you accomplish in the classroom. Student teachers or anyone involved in a job search should think about purchasing a Web site domain and building a Web site. Start your domain name search at one of the many Web sites for domain names. Some of these include Network Solutions located at http://www.networksolutions.com and Register.com located at http://www. register.com. Each Web site enables you to check the availability of your domain.

Examples of Web Site Domains

Kathy Schrock's on-line home page: http://www.kathyschrock.org

Mrs. Perkin's Web site: http://www.mrsperkins.com

Laura Candler's Web site: http://www.lauracandler.com

Reasons for Having Your Own Web Site Domain

- A Web site is great for public relations.
- You have control of how your Web site looks.
- You can update the Web site as often as you like.
- A Web site looks good to a potential employer.
- You can tap your friends or relatives to help you design and update the Web site.
- Your digital filing cabinet is easy to update.

Activity 3

Global Publishing: Getting Started

1. Research and find a Web site domain name that you like (what will appear after www).

   Network Solutions: www.networksolutions.com

   Name Droppers (for researching name options): http://www.namedroppers.com

2. Select and pay for an introductory package. Start small (expect to pay about $20 to $30 each month). Your Internet service provider is a good place to start.

   Host Index is filled with information: http://www.hostindex.com

   Compare Hosts is filled with ideas: http://www.compareWebhosts.com

   Another source is Host compare: http://www.hostcompare.com

3. Reserve your Web site domain through your new Web hosting company. Often, there will be a savings by working through the Web hosting company. In just a few days, you will have your own Web address.

4. Use editing software to start creating your Web site. Free editing software is available to download. A computer store has many options for purchasing editing software.

5. Follow the procedure the Web hosting company sends you to publish your Web site. You are now "on the Web" and ready to showcase your Web site.

SOFTWARE FOR CREATING WEB PAGES ■

Free Software

Netscape

The most popular free software package for creating Web pages is part of the Netscape Communicator Suite. Netscape Composer is free to download at http://channels.netscape.com/ns/browsers/download.jsp

In Netscape, the software is Netscape Composer. This is the software that you will use to create your Web pages.

Open Netscape Composer, and you are ready to start your Web page by just starting to type. After saving the Web page, you can preview it to see what the Web page will look like on-line. You have created your own Web page.

Arachnophilia

Using this software is a quick way to get started. The software does not have many frills and is just a basic editor. You can hyperlink to Web sites and other Web pages. This software is a step up from the template-based Web sites, but it may not be powerful enough if you are creating a large Web site. Many schools use Arachnophilia. This software can be downloaded for free at http://www.arachnoid.com/arachnophilia

Arachnophilia is a powerful Web site workshop. There are many features here for beginners and for those that are more advanced.

Software You May Already Own

To get started, open a word processing document and start typing. Right from this document you can save it as a Web page, and it is ready to be published. Do not worry about fancy graphics or other things. Focus your initial work on the content of the Web site, and other things can come as your skills increase. You may already own the following software.

Microsoft Word

Your word processing program can also be your editor. When you have completed your Web page in Microsoft Word, use the File menu to "Save as Web Page" in HTML. Some of the formatting may shift, but this is a quick and easy way to get started.

Appleworks

Creating Web pages in the Appleworks word processor is also possible. There are a few additional steps to make all your links work, but it can be done. When your Web page is complete, save it as HTML.

Other Software for Creating Web Pages

The Web authoring software of choice for most schools is Microsoft's FrontPage or Macromedia Dreamweaver. Both packages are powerful tools for creating Web pages, as well as organizing and managing the Web site.

■ FINALLY, YOUR VERY OWN ON-LINE DIGITAL FILING CABINET

Now that you have a Web site, it is time to create an on-line digital filing cabinet. Similar to the digital filing cabinet that you created to organize and manage your data documents, this digital filing cabinet needs a clear organization system so that you have a place for everything.

Start basic and easy; changes can always be made at a later date. Do not fuss over clip art, fonts, and backgrounds. Once the information is in the digital filing cabinet, it is easy to enhance the look. My first digital filing cabinet was very basic. Once I needed to add resources, the changes were made slowly.

This very simple table is a good way to start. Use the following table to start sketching out some ideas. Start by selecting four or five main topic areas and list those across the top. Next, list any pages or subtopics below the main heading.

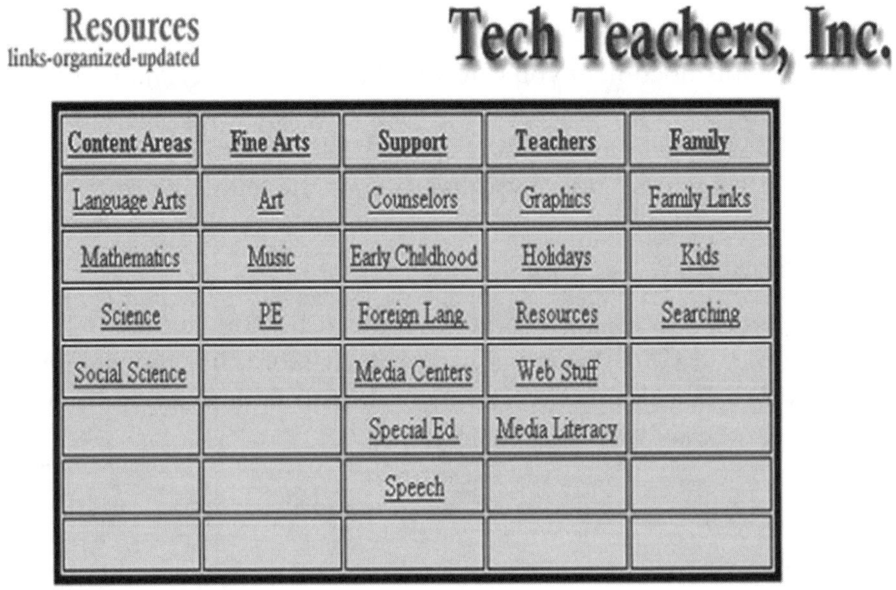

Resources
links-organized-updated

Tech Teachers, Inc.

Content Areas	Fine Arts	Support	Teachers	Family
Language Arts	Art	Counselors	Graphics	Family Links
Mathematics	Music	Early Childhood	Holidays	Kids
Science	PE	Foreign Lang.	Resources	Searching
Social Science		Media Centers	Web Stuff	
		Special Ed.	Media Literacy	
		Speech		

Figure 6.1   My first on-line digital filing cabinet

Activity 4

Planning Guide for an On-line Digital Filing Cabinet

Each of these topic areas that you have identified can become a Web page on your Web site. This table can serve as the master table that links to each Web page.

Adding Resources to the Digital Filing Cabinet

After much rearranging, my digital filing cabinet is filled with hundreds of pages.

Welcome to the Tech Teachers'
Digital Filing Cabinet
Open for You to Explore Anytime!

Curriculum Resources

Language Arts

Reading, Writing, Authors, Literacy Web

Math & Science

Math Web, Weather, ABC website

Social Studies

Geography, History, GPS, Languages Flat Stanley Projects

Teacher Resources

Assessment, Lesson Plans, Curriculum Mapping, Grants, Newsletters, Templates for Teachers, Tutorials, Games CAPI

Integrating Technology

Classroom Management

Differentiating Instruction, Flexible Grouping, Discussion Groups, Study Groups, Planning, Student Resources, e-mail

Data Driven Decision Making

Assessment, Knowledge Management, Standards, Learning Communities, Profiling, Six-Sigma, Grade Book Software

Examples

Webpages, Graphics, Digital File Cabinets Adobe Photo Elements Examples, Playground Build Electronic Portfolios

Technology

Figure 6.2   My digital filing cabinet

The Web pages that you have created are ready for your bookmarks, favorites, or any other Web sites that you are ready to add. Now that the on-line digital filing cabinet has been planned, it is time to create the Web pages and start filling them in with Web sites.

Using your Web-authoring software, create a new Web page and create a chart like the one you drafted. Once the chart has been filled in, save the Web page and create your first subtopic. Label the Web page and save it. Use short file names with no spaces. Continue to create Web pages for the various subcategories.

When all the Web pages have been created, it is time to link the Web pages together. Start with your master table and highlight your first topic. Select the hyperlink symbol or icon and type the URL (Web address) of the location in the dialog box. After the hyperlink is created, it should appear in a blue font as underlined text. Continue to create your hyperlinks for each Web page.

You are ready to add content when the Web pages are linked. Open one of the Web pages, and you are ready to copy and paste Web addresses into the page. An important timesaving step here is to label each of the Web sites so that you remember what they are. Save each Web page as Web addresses are added.

Soon your on-line digital filing cabinet will be filled with resources. The next step is to save all the Web pages and publish the Web site to the selected server. On a school Web server, this may be the technology coordinator's job. Once the Web pages are posted, each will have a unique Web address, and you have published your digital filing cabinet globally.

The last step in the process is to celebrate! You look great on-line. Your resources may help someone else save time, and they are right there on-line, wherever you can get to the Internet.

MOVING FORWARD ■

Organizing and sharing to save time was the focus in this chapter. You now have very specific, useful ways for getting started. Take your time here and make a plan for organizing as you move forward.

Action Plan for Publishing Globally

1. What is your plan to organize Web sites?

2. How do you organize bookmarks or favorites?

3. How do you copy Web site addresses to a word processing document?

4. Based on your Acceptable Use Policy, what can you not post to the Internet?

5. What are your plans for publishing to the Internet?

6. What Web pages would you like to include in your Web site?

7. What software do you plan on using to create your Web page?

8. What are your plans for your on-line digital filing cabinet?

Copyright © 2004 by Corwin Press, Inc. All rights reserved. Reprinted from *Conquering Infoclutter: Timesaving Technology Solutions for Teachers* by Meghan Ormiston. Thousand Oaks, CA: Corwin Press, www.corwinpress.com. Reproduction authorized only for the local school site that has purchased this book.

Focus Questions for Publishing Globally

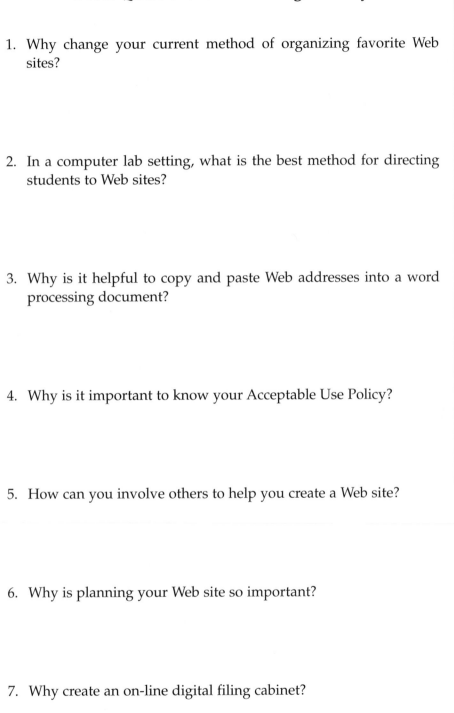

1. Why change your current method of organizing favorite Web sites?

2. In a computer lab setting, what is the best method for directing students to Web sites?

3. Why is it helpful to copy and paste Web addresses into a word processing document?

4. Why is it important to know your Acceptable Use Policy?

5. How can you involve others to help you create a Web site?

6. Why is planning your Web site so important?

7. Why create an on-line digital filing cabinet?

Copyright © 2004 by Corwin Press, Inc. All rights reserved. Reprinted from *Conquering Infoclutter: Timesaving Technology Solutions for Teachers* by Meghan Ormiston. Thousand Oaks, CA: Corwin Press, www.corwinpress.com. Reproduction authorized only for the local school site that has purchased this book.

7

Assessing With Technology

Assessing technology integration projects has unique challenges. Assessment must include the use of the technology tools, as well as the content area evaluation. This chapter looks at ways to effectively assess projects that integrate technology.

Self-
Assessment

Self-Assessment for Evaluation and Technology: Where Are You Now?

1. How can integrated technology lessons be assessed?

2. What tools are available on-line to help with assessment?

3. What is an electronic portfolio?

4. How can games help with assessment?

5. What types of quizzes are available on-line?

6. What tools are available to streamline grading?

Copyright © 2004 by Corwin Press, Inc. All rights reserved. Reprinted from *Conquering Infoclutter: Timesaving Technology Solutions for Teachers* by Meghan Ormiston. Thousand Oaks, CA: Corwin Press, www.corwinpress.com. Reproduction authorized only for the local school site that has purchased this book.

ASSESSMENTS TO MATCH ■
TECHNOLOGY-RICH PROJECTS

WebQuests, technology-rich units, virtual field trips, and on-line research require new assessment methods. Planning to use technology also means planning new assessments. Before students begin a project, the expectations should be clearly defined.

When using authentic assessment tools, students see the real-life connections and expectations of the activity or unit. The expectations are clearly defined and measurable. Students, teachers, and parents have a clear understanding of expectations. A student completing the rubric before turning in the project encourages personal reflection.

One authentic assessment tool to use is a rubric. A good rubric is clearly written and is customized to the lesson. A simple checklist or table can quickly be created, but to save time let us explore some of the rubric Web sites on-line.

Create Rubrics On-line

There are a number of Web sites that simplify the creation of rubrics. These Web sites are filled with many different examples and various categories from which to select. The results are a neatly organized rubric ready to be used in the classroom. The rubrics can be saved and edited or changed in the future.

The following free Web sites save time by providing content ideas and formatting the rubric neatly:

The easy-to-use rubric maker for problem-based learning activities: http://rubistar.4teachers.org

Problem-based learning rubric creator: http://www.4teachers.org/projectbased/checklist.shtml

Background information and examples: http://www.teachervision.com/lesson-plans/lesson-4521.html

Rubrics for all grades: http://www.theeducatorsnetwork.com/utt/rubricsgeneral.htm

Other Ways to Assess Technology-Rich Projects

Many authentic assessment methods can be used to assess technology-rich projects. Assessing the content and the use of technology is very important. Keep in mind that technology is a tool to support teaching and learning. The use of the tool should not be the only thing assessed. Our goal is to integrate curriculum and technology; this should be reflected in the evaluation.

Assessment

	Beginning 1	Development 2	Accomplished 3	Exemplary 4
Speaking Skills	Unable to be heard, no gestures, no eye contact	Difficult to hear, few appropriate gestures, little or no eye contact	Good volume, good gestures, some eye contact	Great voice quality, appropriate gestures, eye contact majority of time
Poetry cube content	Unrelated information used, uncreative approach	Little creativity, lack of sufficient information	Adequate information, some creativity	Extensive material used with support and elaboration, related material used effectively, presenting in an interesting way
Cube creativity	No visual/props	Little creativity, poor effor	Some creativity, some effort, neat appearance	Very creative use of visual/props, neat appearance

Figure 7.1   An example of a rubic for a technology rich project

■ SHOWCASE GREAT PROJECTS USING AN ELECTRONIC PORTFOLIO

Think about the concept of the paper portfolio in a digital form and published on the Internet. Students and teachers can feature their great work and share projects with others. There are many different reasons to create an electronic portfolio. Some of these include:

- Applying to a college or program
- Soliciting new work
- Searching for a job
- Showcasing outstanding projects
- Featuring the artwork, writing, or other digital work of students and teachers

CREATING YOUR ■
OWN ELECTRONIC PORTFOLIO

Electronic portfolios come in all varieties. Basically, a portfolio is created to showcase work in a digital form. Many portfolios are shared on CD-ROMs, on a Web page, or through e-mail. A well-designed electronic portfolio can be saved on the school server, and additions can be made at any time. If this process was started in kindergarten, just imagine the portfolio with which the student would graduate.

Before we discuss how to create an electronic portfolio, think outside of the paper-based portfolios you may have experienced.

- These portfolios can be a dynamic, interactive way to showcase learning.
- Storage of the electronic portfolio is easier than the paper systems.
- Sharing of the portfolio can be done in a variety of ways.
- A group of portfolios can easily be collected and transferred to a new school.
- Students can leave the system with the portfolio saved on one CD instead of pounds of paper.
- The artifacts do not fade, crack, or become dusty.
- You do not have to carry around heavy artifacts in binders.

Decisions

The design is your choice; every portfolio researched looked different. If you can make a Web page, get to work. If you prefer PowerPoint, design it there. Whether using Hyperstudio, MovieWorks, iMovie, or Claris slide show, the software does not matter; people are interested in the content.

On-line Portfolios

The trend today is to post the electronic portfolio on-line on a Web site. This removes any compatibility issues with software or computer platform. Many teachers get lost in design and forget to focus on the content. Plan your content; the best design cannot cover poor content.

My Electronic Portfolio Is On-line

My portfolio is on-line and easy to change. I can quickly add or remove features. My portfolio launches from a graphic with hot links, but the same thing could be done with a table and links to different sections. This is a quick way to share information about what I do and my most recent adventures.

Figure 7.2   My electronic portfolio

What Is Your Electronic Portfolio Plan?

One of the best ways to learn how to create an electronic portfolio is to create one for yourself. Create a Personal Electronic Portfolio today.

Activity 1

Starting Your Personal Electronic Portfolio

1. How would an electronic portfolio be helpful to you?

2. What elements would you like to include in an electronic portfolio?

3. How will you share your electronic portfolio with others?

4. What types of artifacts would you like to include in your electronic portfolio?

5. How will you navigate through your electronic portfolio?

Copyright © 2004 by Corwin Press, Inc. All rights reserved. Reprinted from *Conquering Infoclutter: Timesaving Technology Solutions for Teachers* by Meghan Ormiston. Thousand Oaks, CA: Corwin Press, www.corwinpress.com. Reproduction authorized only for the local school site that has purchased this book.

Job Searching With an Electronic Portfolio

Showcase all that hard work and dazzle someone with your brilliance. An electronic portfolio makes you stand out in a crowd. Many preservice teachers are leaving school armed with an electronic portfolio. Sharing the portfolio with schools can be done by sending a CD-Rom or sending out your Web site address to principals.

Showcase your great work and start creating your electronic portfolio today. If it can be scanned, snapped in a digital picture, or typed, you are ready to go.

■ OTHER TIMESAVING ASSESSMENT TOOLS

There are many tools available to save time with assessment. The most common software is grade book software. This section covers the challenges and benefits of using the grade book software, as well as low cost on-line tools.

Grade Book and Classroom Management Software

Grade Book Programs

Grade book software comes in many forms and is used in many schools worldwide. Many paper-trained teachers are reluctant to try the new software, whereas other teachers could not think of doing things the old way. The general features of grade book software include:

- Record and average students' grades
- Easy to use and modify as needed
- Data manipulation
- Produce reports in a variety of ways

There are many grade book programs, and each program is slightly different, offering a variety of features. There are free programs, individual and network versions, and on-line versions. Most of the programs offer an additional module for looking at grades on-line. Some include Palm Applications for an additional fee.

The latest trend in grade book software is to allow student and parental access to the information over a secure Web site. The parents can log in with a unique password and check on the latest progress. Most parents love this. Many teachers find this helps the students stay on top of the work, as well as promote positive teacher-parent communication.

Another benefit to the on-line grade book is ease of access for teachers. If this module is not currently available to teachers, grades may have to be entered only at school. This on-line feature allows teachers to enter a password and add grades anywhere they can get to the Internet.

With the many commercial programs available, it takes some research to select a program that everyone at school likes. Many of the updated versions enable the information entered into the grade book to flow through to the student's report card which is a big timesaver. Some grade book programs can also be used on a handheld computer, making it quick and easy to add information.

More information can be found online at http://www.techteachers. com/gradebooksoftware.htm

Management Tools

There are a number of class management tools available to help save you time. Most of these tools were originally designed to be used with students and teachers taking on-line courses. Today, some of these features can be found in new statewide portals and portals created in various school districts.

Commercial Sites Although most of these sites were designed to deliver on-line courses, there are many built-in management features at which to look. I like the drop box for assignments. There is a fee to use most of the features. Many of these are being used at the university level. A few examples include:

Blackboard.com: http://www.blackboard.com

WebCt for the higher education market: http://www.Webct.com

Custom Portals A portal is the on-line environment that is created for a specific group. Features may include a place for your on-line digital filing cabinet, links to resources, and areas for chatting and sharing with others, as well as links to standards and assessment information.

School District or Statewide Custom Portals More portals are emerging each year as a way to support teaching and learning. Sharing resources is one benefit as well as providing the tools that teachers need to save time. In most cases, these areas are password protected. Some examples include:

Utah Education Network portals for Utah teachers: http://www.uen. org/tutorial/html/my.uen

Big Chalk: http://www.bigchalk.com/cgi-bin/WebObjects/ WOPortal. woa/db/Home.html

Textbook Companion Assessment

When textbooks are purchased, new options can offer some help with assessment and planning. Some publishers are packaging helpful tools with new textbook adoptions. The tools vary based on the publisher and the grade level for the book. Plan books, customized chapter tests, blackline masters, and Web links are often found on these CD-ROMs.

In addition to the CD-ROMs, many book publishers also have a companion Web site for the textbook. Here you will find links to resources supporting the unit. Many of these are excellent starting points for collecting resources.

You Are Ready to Save Time

You are now armed and ready to try new and exciting management strategies for your classroom. This is an area that will be growing very quickly over the next few years. There will be more new and exciting ways to save time while you manage the many demands in the classroom.

Action Plan for Evaluation and Technology

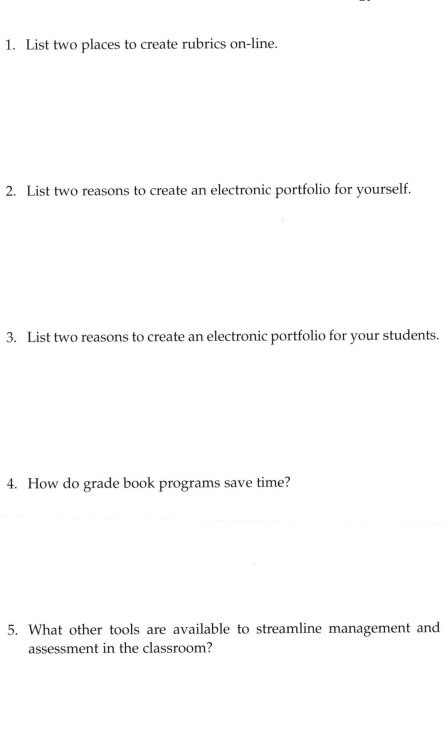

Action Plan

1. List two places to create rubrics on-line.

2. List two reasons to create an electronic portfolio for yourself.

3. List two reasons to create an electronic portfolio for your students.

4. How do grade book programs save time?

5. What other tools are available to streamline management and assessment in the classroom?

Copyright © 2004 by Corwin Press, Inc. All rights reserved. Reprinted from *Conquering Infoclutter: Timesaving Technology Solutions for Teachers* by Meghan Ormiston. Thousand Oaks, CA: Corwin Press, www.corwinpress.com. Reproduction authorized only for the local school site that has purchased this book.

Focus Questions for Evaluation and Technology

1. What types of assessment resources can be found on-line?

2. How can an electronic portfolio be used to boost a child's self-esteem?

3. In what ways can information be shared with parents?

4. How can an electronic portfolio help someone searching for a job?

5. How does the use of games support assessment?

6. How are teachers currently managing grading?

7. What is a portal and how can you use one to help save time?

Copyright © 2004 by Corwin Press, Inc. All rights reserved. Reprinted from *Conquering Infoclutter: Timesaving Technology Solutions for Teachers* by Meghan Ormiston. Thousand Oaks, CA: Corwin Press, www.corwinpress.com. Reproduction authorized only for the local school site that has purchased this book.

8

Connecting Home and School

Communication between home and school is critical. There are many technology tools to help with communication. Parents also suffer from infoclutter and need support to make use of the many technology tools to support home to school communication. Increased communication is the goal. Let us take a look at how we share and communicate information.

Self-
Assessment

Self-Assessment for Connecting
Home and School: Where Are You Now?

1. How are you currently using technology to connect home and school?

2. Specifically, what would you like to learn more about?

3. What roadblocks do you have in your school (no Internet connection, no e-mail)?

4. How is your current communication paper-based?

5. How can technology help save time with communication between home and school?

Copyright © 2004 by Corwin Press, Inc. All rights reserved. Reprinted from *Conquering Infoclutter: Timesaving Technology Solutions for Teachers* by Meghan Ormiston. Thousand Oaks, CA: Corwin Press, www.corwinpress.com. Reproduction authorized only for the local school site that has purchased this book.

CONNECTING HOME AND SCHOOL ■

Teachers worldwide are using technology to increase communication. Parents love to hear about what is going on at school. Send digital pictures to the new group of parents of funny things that happen in class. Go digital and share those great things going on in the classroom.

Some technology tools used by schools today include:

- e-mail
- Newsletters
- e-newsletters
- Homework hotlines
- Voice mail
- Electronic postcards
- Digital photography
- Digital video
- Web cams
- Discussion groups

ELECTRONIC MAIL AS ■ A COMMUNICATION TOOL

Before you embark on an e-mail communication plan, check to see if there are limits set in your district for things sent via e-mail. Check the Acceptable Use Policy regarding e-mail and keep the policy in mind as you share through e-mail. Usually, you need to be careful about sending confidential information via e-mail.

Professional Development

Collect parent e-mail addresses once and create a group. This will simplify communication throughout the year. A quick way to gather parent e-mail addresses is to send home a paper note with your e-mail address. Ask the parents to e-mail you and then copy and paste the parent e-mail address to a class group. This will save you from typing in every parent's e-mail address. This is a great way to save time.

Another way to save time while collecting parents' e-mail addresses is to ask parents to type their preferred e-mail address into a classroom computer when they come in for open house or curriculum night. The timesaving goal is to create a system so that you are not the one typing the e-mail addresses. If you already have a paper copy of the e-mail address list, ask a parent volunteer or older student to type the list into a classroom computer and create an e-mail group for you. This new e-mail group of your parents can be used throughout the year to save you time as you share the great things going on in the classroom.

E-mail is a powerful tool, but we need to remember that not every parent has an e-mail account. Information can be shared about how to acquire a free e-mail address from many of the sources. To accomplish this, a computer can be available before or after parent-teacher conferences or open house with direction and support to set up a free e-mail account. In addition, information can be shared about where to go to check e-mail. The public library or a designated computer at the school may be set up. Some free e-mail sources include:

Yahoo: http://mail.yahoo.com/?.intl=us

Hotmail (Microsoft e-mail; can be viewed in English, as well as French, German, Italian, Japanese, Portuguese (Brazilian), Spanish, Korean, simplified and traditional Chinese, Swedish, and Dutch): www.hotmail.com

■ NEWSLETTERS TO CONNECT HOME AND SCHOOL

Today newsletters can be created using any word processor or desktop publishing program. In our paper-based system, parents may not be getting the news. Many administrators ask teachers to create newsletters and copy them, and they go home to collect dust on kitchen countertops everywhere.

Post Your Class Newsletter On-line

Think about saving the newsletter to your new Web site. Here you can keep an archive, and parents can go back and look at past issues. Grandparents and extended families worldwide can visit the Web site and stay connected. Think about sharing newsletters in exciting new ways.

E-mail Your Newsletter

With a few changes, your newsletter can be e-mailed to parents. Attaching is one option, or you can cut and paste into the e-mail body. Parent e-mail addresses can be stored in a group, and with a quick "Send," off the newsletter goes. If you have hyperlinks in the newsletter, this will keep the links active so that parents can easily click to check out the links.

A combination of print and digital distribution is the reality in many schools. If some parents are connected and check e-mail, that group can be served digitally. Other parents will need paper to keep the lines of communication open. Encouraging parents to try and use digital resources will provide parents with the information they need when they need it, and we can save time at the copy machine.

■ COMMUNICATING HOMEWORK

The homework hotline concept is moving toward putting up assignment pages on the school's Web site. One school has designed a form for teachers to use to quickly update and change as often as needed. Riverside

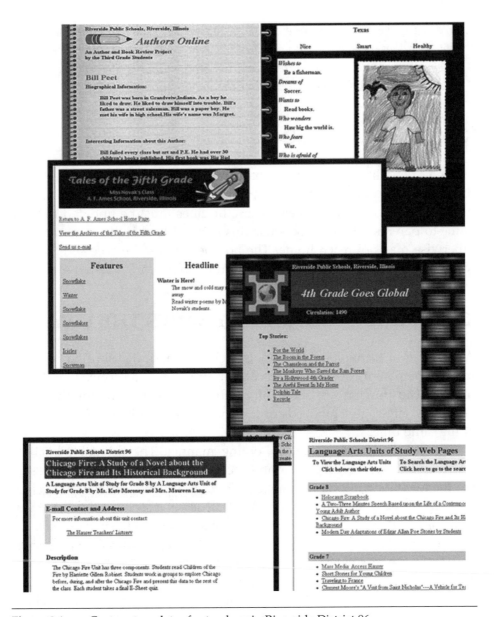

Figure 8.1   Custom templates for teachers in Riverside District 96

Public Schools District #96 is a leader in using custom templates for posting to the school's Web site. Teachers and students can become global publishers quickly and easily. Check out some of the Riverside Public Schools District #96 Auto Forms used at

http://www.techteachers.com/projects2/riversideformsamples.htm

Pete's Active Web Site

One very talented teacher at the middle school level started posting homework assignments on his Web site. To encourage students to visit the Web site and check the homework, Pete added bonus questions that could only be found on-line. Once per week, students could answer the questions through e-mail for extra credit. The parents finally knew what the upcoming homework was and where to go to get review help before a test. The students liked the extra

credit, and the teacher has received thousands of hits each month on the Web site. For those students without Internet and e-mail access at home, the teacher sets up an e-mail address, and the student can access the Web site from any of the computers at school or the public library.

■ HOMEWORK HOTLINE

Homework hotlines are a way to share information about assignments and due dates with parents via the telephone. Most systems are set up as part of the school voice mail system. These hotlines must be updated to be of value to parents. Many schools use this method to share information that otherwise may not reach home. The hotline can also be accessed twenty-four hours per day to help with last minute homework questions.

■ VOICE MAIL TECHNOLOGY SAVES THE DAY

A new use of technology in schools includes mass distribution of voice mail to the parents or staff in the community. This is a service that school districts can purchase to send information out to the community via a voice mail message. Hundreds of telephone calls can be made to families at the same time.

The service works in the following manner. The designated school leader calls a specified number and records the message that is then sent via the telephone to every home identified. Everyone gets the same clear, detailed message within minutes. *My local school district used this last year to notify parents that school would not be in session due to a fire in the school. The students were thrilled, and the parents were relieved when another recorded message sent the next afternoon announced that school would be reopened the next day.*

This is a wonderful technology solution for getting the word out about a snow day or other critical information impacting school. This same technology can be used for staff in place of a telephone tree. There are many vendors that provide the service; so, use your new searching skills to find a perfect match for your school.

■ ELECTRONIC POSTCARDS TO COMMUNICATE IN NEW AND EXCITING WAYS

Use multimedia postcards to share good news with parents. All types are available from Happy Birthday postcards to custom cards to design. The electronic postcards that connect the curriculum are a great way to extend learning. The student fills in the parent's e-mail address, adds a message, and sends the e-mail message. For younger students, a parent volunteer,

Welcome to
Jan Brett's Home Page

Thanks for visiting! Joe and I had a wonderful time going to Arctic for the research for <u>Who's That Knocking on Christmas Eve?</u> Th
I've drawn a Dot to Dot coloring page with the constellations that I remember from watching the sky on our trip. You can find the link to
in the Coloring pages section of this page.

I've created another new coloring page to go with the new Sami Hedgie and the Dot to Dot coloring pages. It's The Ice Bear and the
Coloring pages section.

The 1,000 winning entries in the contest have arrived. Congratulations to everyone! You can find the link to the list of winning schoo

There's a new "All About" letter for Who's that Knocking on Christmas Eve? in the Newsnotes section of my Activities Pages. Joe ar
January of 2001 for the research for the new book. I'd love to tell you a few tidbits about our trip and the new book!

I've added three new bookmarks featuring the Ice Bear from Who's That Knocking on Christmas Eve? You can find the link to the:
"B" in my Activities Pages.

My publisher has announced all of the cities and towns for the fall tour for Who's That Knocking on Christmas Eve? I'll be visiting 21
that you can come. I would love to meet you! There's a complete list in the 2002 Tour link on this page.

Figure 8.2   Jan Brett's site is filled with creative ways to communicate

senior citizen helper, or older student can help the younger student with the electronic postcard. Check out PE postcards from P.E. Central which can be located at

http://www.pecentral.org/postcard/postcardmenu.html

Additional Web Sites for E-cards

Free nature e-cards: http://www.e-cards.com

Free Yahoo e-cards: http://greetings.yahoo.com

Free Funbrain e-cards for kids: http://www2.funbrain.com/cgi-bin/ecard.cgi? Author and illustrator Jan Brett's collection: http://www.janbrett.com/vcards

Great collection for a small annual fee: http://free.bluemountain.comJ

Jan Brett Makes Connecting With Home More Beautiful

This is my favorite Web site to share parent communication tied to the curriculum or time of year. Jan Brett's artwork is amazing, and her

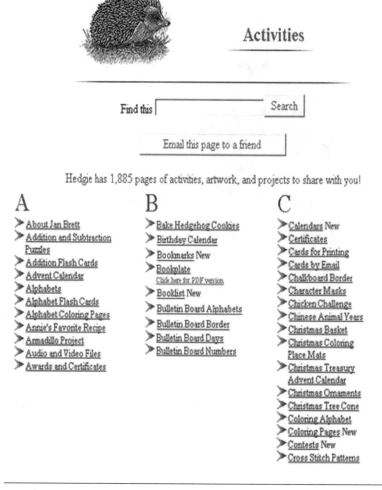

Figure 8.3   Activities found on Jan Brett's site

Web site is filled with digital resources to be used across the curriculum. This is a very active Web site that is always changing with new pages and activities added each week. The current count in the activities section is approximately 2,000 activities, projects, and artwork to share. The Web site address is http://www.janbrett.com

■ DIGITAL IMAGES SHARED WITH PARENTS

Parents love to see pictures of students at work in school. Use a digital camera or have your film developed and put on a CD-ROM. Another way to share images digitally is to scan the image on a scanner that is connected to the computer. By making the images digital, the same image can be used in the school newsletter, sent home through e-mail, printed for the bulletin board, used in your curriculum night presentation, or included on an about the author page. There are many exciting ways to use digital images at school.

Digital Photography

Digital cameras are becoming a tool available in schools. Digital cameras do not use film or other consumables. Point and click the camera and download the pictures into the computer. These digital pictures can then be treated like clip art and placed in documents, e-mail, on the bulletin board, or the Web site. Sharing pictures digitally is as simple as attaching a file. Catch that student doing something good and share it.

Student-Created Video

Students worldwide are creating videos that are capable of being shared over the Internet. The price of this technology has decreased in the past few years, opening the doors to new creative ways of sharing information. Armed with a digital camcorder and editing software, students and teachers can quickly and easily create videos to share. Some of the best on-line examples can be found at

http://www.techteachers.com/multimedia.htm

Web Cams

Although they are not quite ready for prime time, a few teachers are exploring the use of Web cams in classrooms. The Web cam is mounted in the classroom, and the pictures can be viewed on the Internet. The use of a Web cam in a classroom may not fit with your district's Acceptable Use Policy and may not broadcast to the outside world from behind your firewall.

DISCUSSION GROUPS AND ■ PARENT COMMUNITIES ON-LINE

Chat Rooms for Parents

Some educators are also involving families in on-line communities. This can take many forms, but all are designed to bring the community together by sharing information. Some districts have a chat room for members of their community. This is a relatively new way to use the technology, but as schools work to involve their communities, exciting changes will take place.

There are many special Web sites for parents to share information and learn from one another on-line. There are so many places to collect and share information on-line. I investigated chat rooms and bulletin board posting sites, as well as informational Web sites for parents. There is something for everyone. Here are a few major Web sites that we discovered:

http://www.parentsplace.com/messageboards — This Web site is filled with hundreds of bulletin boards and chat rooms. Very specific groups have been formed, and many of them are very active. This Web site is part of the ivillage.com Web family.

http://www.parentsoup.com/boards — Parent soup is another of the ivillage.com communities serving parents. This is a favorite Web site filled with resources and bulletin boards for parents.

Special Needs Communities

http://www.chadd.org/webpage.cfm?cat_id=7&subcat_id=39 — This Web site is for children and adults with attention deficit hyperactivity disorder. This organization has a very active Web site filled with information. This link will take you to the chat pages of the Web site. About once per month an expert is on-line chatting with members of the group. This is a great way to share information with a group.

http://www.ldonline.org — This Web site, designed for use with parents and teachers, is filled with information about learning disabilities.

■ CHAT ROOMS FOR STUDENTS

Most schools do not allow chatting on-line at school, but at home many students are chatting on-line for hours. Many of them chat on-line while talking on the telephone. Don Tapscott wrote about this in his book *Growing Up Digital: The Rise of the Net Generation*. This book is an excellent look at how students are using technology in their lives. This book was written in collaboration with over 300 students worldwide. The students came together in a protected chat area to share feelings and help Don Tapscott put together his thoughts on growing up digital. The companion Web site for the book is http://www.growing updigital.com

Students and E-mail

At home, students are using e-mail to communicate with friends, teachers, and sometimes strangers. It is important for parents to know what children and young adults are doing on-line. Some important things to remember include:

- Never give your name or contact information.
- Never agree to meet someone you have met on-line face-to-face.
- Parents should get to know the Internet services children use.
- Never respond to anything inappropriate.
- Report anything inappropriate to parents immediately.

More safety information can be found on the following Web sites:

The leader for on-line safety for children: http://www.safekids.com

From the University of Oklahoma Police Department: http://www.ou.edu/oupd/kidtool.htm

The Children's Partnership: http://www.childrenspartnership.org/bbar/safety.html

COMMUNICATE TO SAVE TIME ■

Communication is what it is all about. Technology tools can help you with the communication process, but critical timesaving procedures need to be in place. This chapter is filled with links to share with parents, teachers, administrators, and students. Make the most of the communication tools you already have.

Action Plan for Connecting Home and School

1. List three ways e-mail can be used to communicate between home and school.

    a.

    b.

    c.

2. Specifically, how can your newsletters be improved?

    a.

    b.

    c.

3. How can e-mail postcards help connect home and school?

4. How can video be used to connect home and school?

5. What are some ways to use technology to communicate homework expectations?

6. Specifically, what are your plans to improve home and school communication?

    a.

    b.

    c.

Copyright © 2004 by Corwin Press, Inc. All rights reserved. Reprinted from *Conquering Infoclutter: Timesaving Technology Solutions for Teachers* by Meghan Ormiston. Thousand Oaks, CA: Corwin Press, www.corwinpress.com. Reproduction authorized only for the local school site that has purchased this book.

Focus Questions for Connecting Home and School

Focus Questions

1. Why is it important to connect home and school?

2. What is happening currently in schools to improve home and school connections?

3. How can e-mail be used to connect home and school?

4. How does technology help with the recordkeeping of correspondence?

5. What are some of the newer technology tools that are found in schools today?

6. What benefits do you expect with improved home and school communication?

Copyright © 2004 by Corwin Press, Inc. All rights reserved. Reprinted from *Conquering Infoclutter: Timesaving Technology Solutions for Teachers* by Meghan Ormiston. Thousand Oaks, CA: Corwin Press, www.corwinpress.com. Reproduction authorized only for the local school site that has purchased this book.

9

Integrating Technology and Curriculum

TOOLS TO HELP ■ INTEGRATE TECHNOLOGY ACROSS THE CURRICULUM

Technology tools should be in classrooms and integrated throughout the day. Teachers and students need access to powerful tools to make the most of teaching and learning. Unlimited access to information resources will allow all students and teachers to realize the dream of learning anytime and anyplace.

Computers should be in the classroom. With computers in the class-rooms, a teacher can easily integrate technology into the curriculum. From one computer, to one computer for each student, the teacher needs tools that are stable and ready to use at any moment.

Professional Development

Unfortunately, I often see technology misused in schools. Computer labs are filled with students using the same drill and practice software week after week. Disjointed activities are planned without linking to curriculum, and computer labs are filled with students typing term papers for weeks on end. Technology in schools should be one tool to support teaching and learning tied to the curriculum. This chapter looks at specifics to help with integration.

Self-
Assessment

Self-Assessment for Integrating Technology Across the Curriculum: Where Are You Now?

1. How is technology integrated in your school?

2. In what content areas are you currently integrating technology and curriculum?

3. What roadblocks have you faced while integrating technology?

4. What professional development do you need to better integrate technology?

5. What support do you need to better integrate technology?

6. Specifically, where do you want to start to integrate technology?

Copyright © 2004 by Corwin Press, Inc. All rights reserved. Reprinted from *Conquering Infoclutter: Timesaving Technology Solutions for Teachers* by Meghan Ormiston. Thousand Oaks, CA: Corwin Press, www.corwinpress.com. Reproduction authorized only for the local school site that has purchased this book.

■ THE ONE-COMPUTER CLASSROOM

One computer in the classroom can be a very powerful teaching and learning tool. Many things can be done on one computer by rotating students throughout the day and planning independent and small group activities that tie into the curriculum. Problem-solving and critical thinking activities can also be supplemented with appropriate drill and practice. Connected to the Internet, the computer can also serve as a classroom reference library.

As a classroom teacher, I had a one-computer classroom. I did my best to rotate students and keep things rolling. Large screen televisions were installed a few years later, making that one computer a true teaching and learning station. On the large screen monitor, the entire class could see the computer at once. With a large television or monitor permanently mounted in the classroom, teachers come to depend on this technology, as they create lesson plans and discover new ways to weave technology into subject areas.

Many schools do not have the luxury of large screen monitors in every classroom. Televisions or projectors are rolled on carts between classrooms. A sign-out procedure for equipment is a start, but teachers cannot depend on the equipment being available, leaving technology integration to chance as they plan lesson plans. In every building using this method, you always have the "technology hogs." These are the staff members who sign out the equipment and adopt it as their own. This happens in every building, not just yours.

LCD projectors and monitors are another way to make the most of the one-computer classroom. These projectors are great for large presentations. The text and graphics are usually very clear and easy to read. Some updated schools have LCD projectors mounted on the ceiling in a computer lab or auditorium. These LCD projectors are still expensive, and the replacement bulbs run in the hundreds of dollars. The ability to project what is on the screen is critical in the one-computer classroom.

■ CLASSROOM COMPUTERS VERSUS THE LAB ENVIRONMENT

Much has been written on this subject. This is a hot topic in most schools. I agree with many of the leading experts that computers should be in the classroom, not in a central location. I agree because I see a great misuse of computer labs in scheduling, support, and connection to the curriculum.

The great scheduling debate occurs in most schools. Curriculum connections are difficult to plan if you cannot get into the computer lab because of scheduling conflicts. Some schools solve this conflict by scheduling all students into the computer lab for a set number of minutes per week. This is where we see the biggest misuse of the computer lab.

In many schools, teachers bring students to the computer lab for another teacher or aide to instruct them on a program or a project. In most cases, this has little to do with the curriculum being covered in the classroom.

Many classroom teachers are not part of the instruction in the computer lab because it is grouped with special area subjects such as gym, art, music, and so forth. Teachers feel the students are getting technology, and they do not need any beyond those few minutes per week. If we want to make the most of technology tools at school, we need to change how and where our students are accessing technology.

Experiments are going on everywhere in schools. Rows of computers are added to classrooms. Think about what you could do with four or five computers in your classroom. Some teams of teachers share computers located in a central location close to their classrooms. In a few lucky classrooms and in some states, students have their own laptop computers.

MOBILE COMPUTING SOLUTIONS ■

Laptop Computers

As computers get smaller, many opportunities open up for schools. Laptop computer carts are found in some schools today. These laptop computer carts hold as many as thirty laptop computers, and the power management is built-in, making it possible to charge the laptop computers when they are stored in the laptop computer cart.

Many of these laptop computer carts are equipped with a wireless network connection. Each laptop computer has a network card, and the network cards communicate with the network and the Internet through the wireless hub. No wires are needed. Roll the cart in and start integrating. This is a great solution for a school without the space for a computer lab full of desktop computers.

Other Mobile Solutions

Smart keyboards have been in many schools for years. These keyboards are smaller and lighter than laptop computers and are designed for word processing. The keyboards talk to the printer through an infrared port located in back or a USB cable. Prices vary on these; the range I found was $200 to $400. Two brand names to look for are Alphasmart and Dreamwriter. There is a new Alphasmart, the Dana, which runs the Palm operating system.

Portable Digital Assistants (PDAs) Go to School

Many schools are exploring the use of handheld computers, better known as portable digital assistants. The affordable and powerful handheld computers may be perfect for the school setting. A few schools are leading the way in how handheld computers can be used in a variety of disciplines. In science, many schools are using handheld computers with scientific probes to gather and interpret data.

■ INFUSING TECHNOLOGY ACROSS THE CURRICULUM

Professional Development

Teachers need support to infuse technology across the curriculum, as well as help with the actual hardware and software. Districts struggle to staff positions to best support teaching and learning. There is no one perfect solution, but a very important discussion for each building.

Technology must be integrated into the curriculum, not seen as an "add-on." The purpose of technology in the classroom is to support teaching and learning. Technology does not stand alone, and we should not "do" technology for thirty minutes once per week. Technology is a tool. Just as the chalkboard, overhead, textbooks, and audiovisual equipment are considered tools of our trade, so, too, should technology.

This integration section was designed as a starting point, a springboard, to your planning and thinking about new ways to support teaching and learning with technology. In many cases, I have included a completed sample and also a reproducible blackline master. Many more examples can be found on-line.

Most of the samples included in the following sections can be created using the software you already have on your computer. This is just a small sample of the hundreds more that you can find on the companion Web site to this book. I will be adding new ideas and updating the Web site periodically.

The one additional piece of software that I find helpful at all grade levels and content areas is Inspiration software. Inspiration and Kidspiration (for younger children) software enable you to simply and easily create maps, charts, and graphic organizers. The software enables quick and easy addition of ideas as the group brainstorms. Graphics, color, and other enhancements can also be added. Many examples and more information can be found on-line at the Inspiration home page located at

http://www.inspiration.com

Inspiration samples can be found at

http://www.inspiration.com/vlearning/index.cfm?fuseaction=example

■ LANGUAGE ARTS INTEGRATION IDEAS

Technology integration in language arts goes far beyond the word processor. Students can now collaborate on writing projects with someone halfway across the world or in the next town. There are many ways for students to write for a new audience. Students and teachers have many new opportunities to communicate information in new ways.

My Story Map

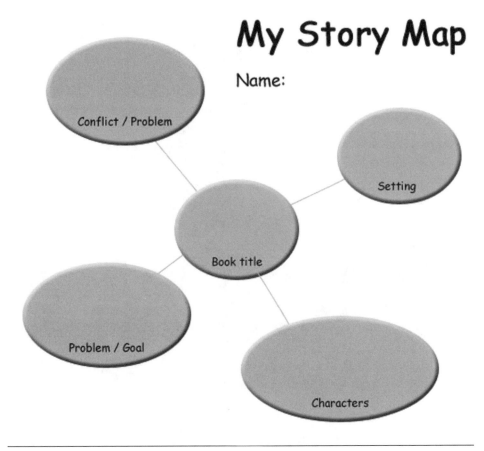

Name:

Conflict / Problem

Setting

Book title

Problem / Goal

Characters

Figure 9.1   An example of a story map

Students and teachers need information literacy skills to better understand how to find and use the information they find on-line. Cut-and-paste plagiarism is everywhere. Everyone needs to understand what can and cannot be used and how to cite resources.

There are many ways to incorporate technology into the language arts curriculum. Use the one computer in the classroom to brainstorm topics and ideas. These can then be saved and used throughout the unit.

Story Maps

This is an example of a primary story map created in a word processing program or a drawing program. Young students can use simple words or draw pictures in each of the sections. This same story map can be adapted for all curricular areas. To simplify recreating this example, a simple table in a word processing document can be created.

Author Studies

Studying the life of an author is a natural extension of reading. Many author Web sites can be found, along with WebQuests and projects

Figure 9.2   An author WebQuest created as a whole school project

that other teachers have created. Some authors may respond to a class e-mail, and others offer activities and extensions of stories on-line. A few examples are listed here with many more organized on the Web site. The following example of a Web site about authors can be found at

http://www.ottawaelem.lasall.k12.il.us/OES%20folder/OES/OES%20Webquest%202002/McKinley2002/authors/McKinleyIntro/McKinleyintro.html

A talented team of third grade teachers created a third grade author study and book review project. This unit was created several years ago and is updated each year as third graders participate in the project. There are on-line links to over thirty authors at the third grade level.

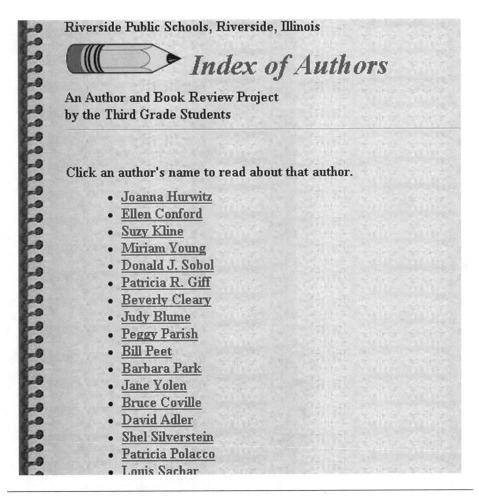

Riverside Public Schools, Riverside, Illinois

Index of Authors

**An Author and Book Review Project
by the Third Grade Students**

Click an author's name to read about that author.

- Joanna Hurwitz
- Ellen Conford
- Suzy Kline
- Miriam Young
- Donald J. Sobol
- Patricia R. Giff
- Beverly Cleary
- Judy Blume
- Peggy Parish
- Bill Peet
- Barbara Park
- Jane Yolen
- Bruce Coville
- David Adler
- Shel Silverstein
- Patricia Polacco
- Louis Sachar

Figure 9.3   Book Review Project

The lesson plan with detailed information and an on-line rubric can be located at

http://www.district96.w-cook.k12.il.us/units/languagearts/pages/2088.2.15.01.html

Read some of the reviews found on-line at

http://www.district96.w-cook.k12.il.us/gr3reviews/index.html

Poetry

Figure 9.4 shows a bio poem written by a fourth grader. The students in this school cannot use their own names when publishing work on the school Web site. Each student in this class has selected the name of a state as a "pen name." This "pen name" will be used throughout the year instead of the student's name. Be sure to check your Acceptable Use Policy before posting student work on the school Web site.

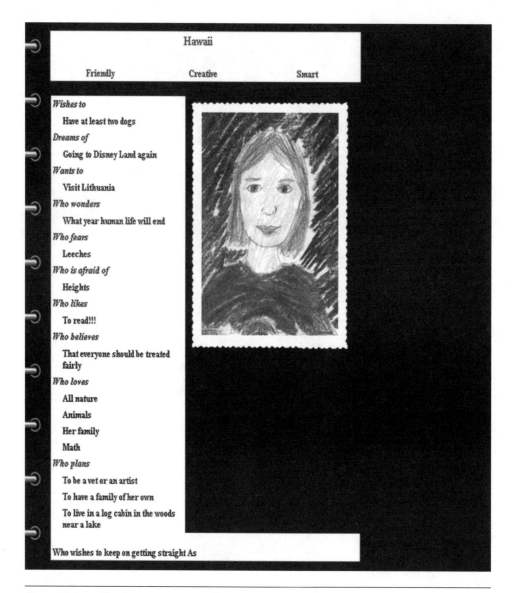

Figure 9.4 Student poetry posted on a custom template

ABC Web Site

This Web site (Figure 9.5) was created by my son (with a little help from me) when he was a kindergarten student. He has difficulty with his fine motor skills; so instead of writing an ABC book, we created a multi-media ABC book. This example can be found on-line at

http://www.techteachers.com/abcweb/abc/index.htm

As a six-year-old, he went to school and shared his new Web site with his class. My son selected each font and color for the opening pages, typed each sentence (using inventive spelling), and then recorded the sentence on each page. This project could be done in the classroom on any topic with each student completing a page of the book.

Figure 9.5   Patrick's ABC book

SCIENCE INTEGRATION IDEAS ■

Fourth Graders Tackling Tough Issues

A talented team of fourth grade teachers created this collaborative Fourth Grade Goes Global project (Figure 9.6). Each year the students write about environmental issues, and their stories are published in one place on the school Web site.

Inquiry Charts

This simple inquiry chart (Figure 9.7) can be modified to match most units of study. This is a good way for students to organize information that they gather while researching. The inquiry chart can be created using a table in a word processing document or a spreadsheet program. This organizational tool is also a good way to help students break down research into their own words, one strategy to cut down on cut-and-paste plagiarism.

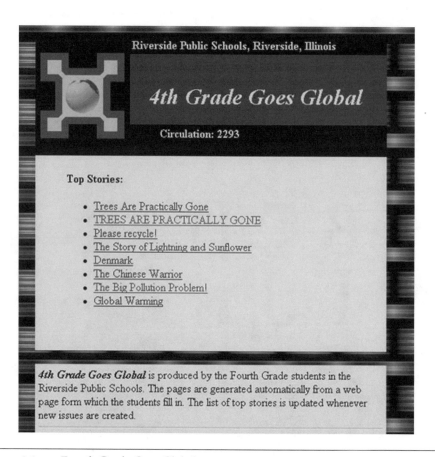

Figure 9.6   Fourth Grade Goes Global

Castle Name	Location	History	Notable Sites Within Castle	Web Resources
Appleby Castle				
Durham Castle				
Windsor Castle				
Kendall Castle				

Figure 9.7   An example of an inquiry chart

Our project was created to help students better understand rivers.

Figure 9.8   A school-wide WebQuest

The River Project

This is a building-wide project based on the theme "Rivers." Each grade level worked together to create a WebQuest or unit of study that aligned to the curriculum. The teachers became global publishers by posting this project on the school Web site, sharing their ideas and lessons with the world. This project can be found on-line at

http://www.ottawaelem.lasall.k12.il.us/OES%20folder/OES/OES%20Webquest%202002/Central2002/central/!central.htm

Growth of My Plant

Using a simple spreadsheet, students of all ages can add information and create various types of graphs. The following example is an extension of a science lesson and is a good way to show growth over time.

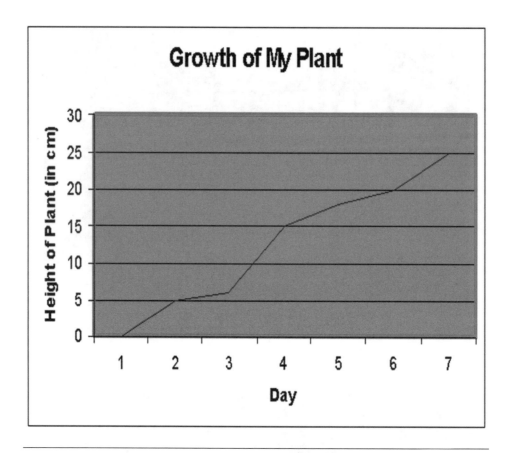

Figure 9.9   The growth of My Plant created in a spread sheet

■ SOCIAL STUDIES INTEGRATION IDEAS

You can consult with on-line experts, visit virtual museums, follow on-line adventures, and study cultures of the world with the click of your mouse. There is so much from which to select. Use your new advanced searching skills to save time and quickly get to what you need.

Research Organizer

For example, research organizers can be used to help students focus on critical events in history. The research organizer can be created in a word processing program using text boxes and lines. Clip art and graphics can also be added. A simple research organizer can be used to help students make sense of events in history.

A simple table with selected headings can help students organize research and keep track of resources used. Creating and using tools like this is a great way to stop the cut-and-paste plagiarism found in so many research reports today.

Castle Fortifications Project

A Web Quest in Social Science for Group.
by <u>Mrs. Byland</u>

Riverside Public Schools, Riverside,
Illinois

<u>Introduction</u> | <u>Task</u> | <u>Process</u> | <u>Information Sources</u> | <u>Evaluation</u> | <u>Conclusion</u>

Introduction

"Hey Henrich! Do you know of a good castle builder around here?" asked
Wilfred of Cornwall.

You are the owner of a construction company in the Middle Ages and can
certainly help this man with his needs. In this project you will be able to assist
many future customers with your skills in castle building.

Task

You will create a business flyer
to display your previous castle
constructions. These will
introduce yourself and your
company to future customers.

The flyer will define a list of

Figure 9.10   A Castle WebQuest

Castle WebQuest

WebQuests can be used across the curriculum. Many examples can be
found on-line, including the following example by a junior high teacher.
The complete WebQuest can be found on-line at

http://www.district96.w-cook.k12.il.us/Webquests/quests/
bylandc6castles.html

MATHEMATICS INTEGRATION IDEAS ■

WebQuests, spreadsheet activities, collaborative projects, writing for
a new audience, and ask an expert are just a few of the ways to use
technology with mathematics. I have created a mathematics and technology
Web site for teachers that is filled with resources. The virtual manipulatives
are a wonderful way to use technology in the mathematics classroom.
My mathematics Web site can be found on-line at

http://www.techteachers.com/mathematics.htm

Stephen's Checkbook

DESCRIPTION	CREDIT	DEBIT	TOTAL
Get allowance	10.00		10.00
buy candy		2.50	7.50
fix bike tire		5.00	2.50
get allowance	10.00		12.50

Figure 9.11   Create a table to record and add amounts

Spreadsheets Support Problem Solving

Spreadsheets are a powerful tool in the mathematics classroom. Students in kindergarten can use simple spreadsheets to record data and create charts. Students in the upper grades can use very sophisticated spreadsheets to solve problems. There are many problems that can be solved using a spreadsheet at all grade levels.

Mathematics WebQuests

A talented eighth grade mathematics team worked together to create the following WebQuest. This collaborative unit was created using an on-line lesson plan form. By posting this lesson on the school Web site, the teachers all know where the lesson can be found on-line, and the lesson is available to others that may like to use it. This school district finds this very helpful as teachers' assignments shift from year to year. The address for this lesson is

http://www.district96.w-cook.k12.il.us/hauser/math/perfectspace/index.html

Riverside Public Schools District 96

Millionaire Mania

A Mathematics Unit of Study for Grade 8

E-mail Contact and Address

For more information about this unit contact:

Hauser School Email

Description

You have just won $1,000,000! In order to be able to keep the money you must spend exactly $1,000,000 on a minimum of 15 items and a maximum of 50. In order to keep track of your spending you are to create a spreadsheet. This project will give you the opportunity to experience just how large a million dollars is and how to create a spreadsheet with the appropriate columns to make this task much easier. The requirements are listed below. Good luck and happy spending!

Keywords

These keywords have been entered to help this page to be found by a search.

spreadsheet middle school tax

Objectives of the Unit

Students will develop formulas to calculate tax, running totals, and balance left to spend on items purchased towards spending exactly $1,000,000. Students will use computer spreadsheet to accomplish the objective.

Students will use internet to search for items to purchase.

Students will summarize experience and advantages of spreadsheet usage

---

Figure 9.12   A Math WebQuest "Millionaire Mania"

THIS IS JUST A SAMPLE ■

This collection of integration ideas is just a tiny sample from the thousands of projects linked off the companion Web site located at www.infoclutter. com. On-line you will find links to lessons and resources for all teachers in all subjects. From foreign language to physical education, there are links and resources organized in a digital filing cabinet. Check the Web site for the up-to-the-minute collection.

Action Plan for Integrating Technology Across the Curriculum

1. Who can you turn to for support when using technology?

2. Why are classroom computers important?

3. What are some things to consider when planning to integrate technology across the curriculum?

4. How is technology hardware arranged in your school?

5. If a computer lab is available, how is it currently used?

6. Specifically, list three projects you would like to try.

   a.

   b.

   c.

7. What on-line resources would you like to explore in more depth?

Focus Questions for Integrating Technology Across the Curriculum

1. Why integrate technology across the curriculum?

2. What support do teachers need?

3. How is technology organized in schools today?

4. Other than computers, what technology tools are available in schools?

Copyright © 2004 by Corwin Press, Inc. All rights reserved. Reprinted from *Conquering Infoclutter: Timesaving Technology Solutions for Teachers* by Meghan Ormiston. Thousand Oaks, CA: Corwin Press, www.corwinpress.com. Reproduction authorized only for the local school site that has purchased this book.

Bibliography

Hemphill, B. (1989). *Taming the paper tiger.* Washington, DC: Hemphill & Assoc.

Marzano, R., Whisler, J. S., Dean, C. B., & Pollock, J. E. (2000). *Research into practice series: Effective instructional practices in the classroom.* Aurora, CO: Mid-continent Research for Education and Learning. Retrieved May 1, 2003, from http://www.mcrel.org

McCain, T., & Jukes, I. (2001). *Windows on the future.* Thousand Oaks, CA: Corwin Press.

McTighe, J., & Wiggins, G. (1998). *Understanding by design.* Alexandria, VA: ASCD.

Morgenstern, J. (1998). *Organizing from the inside out: The foolproof system for organizing your home, your office, and your life.* New York: Henry Holt & Company.

November, A. (2001). *Empowering students with technology.* Arlington Heights, IL: SkyLight Professional Development.

Sylwester, R. (1995). *A celebration of neurons: An educator's guide to the human brain.* Alexandria, VA: ASCD.

Tapscott, D. (1998). *Growing up digital: The rise of the net generation.* New York: McGraw-Hill.

Tomlinson, C. A. (1999). *The differentiated classroom: Responding to the needs of all learners.* Alexandria, VA: Association for Supervision and Curriculum Development.

Wolfe, P. (2001). *Brain matters: Translating research into classroom practice.* Alexandria, VA: ASCD.

Index